Data Quality

Data Quality

The Field Guide

Thomas C. Redman, Ph.D.

Digital Press
An Imprint of Elsevier
Boston • Oxford • Auckland • Johannesburg • Melbourne • New Delhi

Digital Press™ is an imprint of Elsevier

A member of the Reed Elsevier group

Permissions may be sought directly from Elsevier's Science and Technology Rights Department in
Oxford, UK. Phone: (44) 1865 843830, Fax: (44) 1865 853333, e-mail: permissions@elsevier.co.uk.
You may also complete your request on-line via the Elsevier homepage: http://www.elsevier.com by
selecting "Customer Support" and then "Obtaining Permissions".

Recognizing the importance of preserving what has been written, Butterworth–Heinemann
prints its books on acid-free paper whenever possible.

Butterworth–Heinemann supports the efforts of American Forests and the
Global ReLeaf program in its campaign for the betterment of trees, forests, and
our environment.

The images used herein were obtained from IMSI's MasterClips/MasterPhotos© Collection, 1895
East Francisco Blvd., San Rafael, CA 94901-5506, USA.

Library of Congress Cataloging-in-Publication Data

Redman, Thomas C.
   Data quality : the field guide / by Thomas Redman.
      p. cm.
   Includes index.
   ISBN 1-55558-251-6 (pbk. : alk. paper)
      1. Database management—Quality control. I. Title.

QA76.9.D3 R425 2000
005.74--dc21

                                    00-047513

British Library Cataloging-in-Publication Data

A catalogue record for this book is available from the British Libary.

The publisher offers special discounts on bulk orders of this book.
For information, please contact:

Manager of Special Sales
Butterworth–Heinemann
225 Wildwood Avenue
Woburn, MA 01801-2041
Tel: 781-904-2500
Fax: 781-904-2620

For information on all Butterworth–Heinemann publications available, contact our World Wide
Web home page at: http://www.bh.com.

10 9 8 7 6 5 4 3 2

Printed in the United States of America

For Nancy

Contents

Foreword   xi
Preface   xiii
Author's Note   xv
Acknowledgments   xvii

Part A: Who Cares About Data Quality?   1

1   Yes, Millie, Even CEOs Are Interested in Data Quality   3

2   Internet Users Wonder, "Are These Prices Correct?" . . . and Dot.Coms Better Make Sure They Are   7

3   Chief Financial Officers and Managers of Ongoing Operations Need to Know "Where the Money Is"   15

4   Marketers Need to Know about Their Customers   21

5   Chief Information Officers Are Stuck in the Middle   27

6   Just in Case You Didn't See Yourself in Chapters 1–5   35

Part B: The Business Case for Data Quality   37

7   Disasters Played Out in Public   39

8   Poor Data Quality Can Be Insidious   43

9   Seek Competitive Advantage Through Quality Data   47

Part C: The Heart of the Matter   51

10   A Database Is Like a Lake   53

11   Likely Outcomes   57

12   The Organic Nature of Data   61

13   Crafting the Approach   65

Part D: Necessary Background   69

14   Data and Data Quality Defined   71

15   Second-Generation Data Quality Systems   75

16   The Customer-Supplier Model   95

Part E: Blocking and Tackling   99

17   Understanding Customer Needs
     (After All, They Are the Final Arbiters of Quality)   101

18   Better, Faster, Cheaper   107

19   Measurement 2: Data Tracking   113

20   Edit Controls   119

21   Statistical Control: Establishing a Basis for Prediction   123

22   Quality Improvement: Root Cause Analysis to
     Uncover the Real Causes of Error   131

23   Quality Planning—Setting Targets for Improvement   137

24   Quality Planning—Designing New Information Chains   141

25   A Note on Reengineering   147

Part F: Middle Management Roles and Responsibilities   151

26   Data Supplier Management   153

27   Managing Information Chains   161

28   Making Better Decisions   167

29   Tools   171

Part G: Why Senior Management Must Lead
and What It Must Do   175

30   Senior Leadership and Support   177

31   Crafting a Data Policy   181

32   Organizing for Data Quality   187

33   Recognizing Social Issues   189

34   Advancing the Data Culture   197

Part H: Summaries **203**

35	On and Just Over the Horizon	205
36	Field Tips Reorganized	209
	Appendix: The United States Elections of 2000	217
	Glossary	221
	References	229
	Instructions for Downloading Figures and Tables	231
	Index	233

Foreword

The economy is undergoing enormous upheaval. New business models are being developed and tested. Dot.coms spring up seemingly in real time. "Bricks and mortars" are striking back. The pace of globalization quickens. And companies merge and split themselves like never before. One moment the investment community simply demands a good idea and good people, the next it demands immediate profit. No one knows how or where all this activity will lead, or even if it will ever slow down, never mind stop.

But one trend is clear enough. The "new economy" already runs on data and the importance of data will only grow. The "old economy" depended on data too, but nowhere near to the same degree. Today a company's data are right there on its Web site, for all to see and use, or study and criticize. The stakes are enormous.

Both as consumers and as managers we are deluged, even glutted, with data. And the quantities of data can only grow. This trend portends an ever-increasing need for data of extremely high quality. Consumers need to trust the companies with whom they do business. In the old economy, they developed this trust through personal interactions with companies' representatives. Now those interactions are no more than data going back and forth. And a consumer will simply not trust a company that provides bad data.

Similarly, managers and decision makers need to trust the data on which they base decisions. Otherwise they rely on intuition alone. But the pace of change and the consequences of being "wrong" are simply too great for intuition to be the sole basis of decisions. Decision makers need timely, correct, pertinent *facts*.

Financial performance demands high-quality data. The operational costs that stem from simple data errors are simply too great. New dot.coms especially need to show that they can run credible businesses and make money.

They, more than others, cannot waste the time and money it takes to find and fix errors and to make good on the problems those errors cause.

Achieving high-quality data, and reaping the business rewards, is at once difficult and easy. It is extremely difficult when personal and organizational infighting intrudes. At the same time, deep in their hearts everyone knows that "data quality" is the right thing to do. So it can be easy, once the political barriers are lowered.

Tom Redman provides the needed prescriptions herein. He helps all of us understand the opportunity. He alerts managers to the most common political issues. He explains where accountability for data must lie and he provides the "how-to's" so people can do what is necessary. This is important stuff. And it works.

Jay Walker
Chief Executive Officer
Walker Digital
Greenwich, CT
September, 2000

Preface

Clearly, the Information Age has arrived. Huge databases, the Internet, and sophisticated communications networks combine to make more and different kinds of data readily accessible. And technology promises even more. Companies are using the Internet to dramatically alter supply chains. They are using data mining techniques to customize their offerings to individual customers. And "knowledge management" has acquired a certain cache, as companies struggle to truly become Information Age companies.

If Information Technologies are the engines of the Information Age, then data and information are the fuels. Most people don't think much about data. Data are simply the "stuff in those computers" or the "ingredients to this quarterly report." But clearly, without the right fuel, the engine will sputter and the organization won't go anywhere.

This *Field Guide* focuses on the quality of Information Age fuels—namely data. Unfortunately, the quality of data and information created and used by almost all organizations is low. When they think about it, almost everyone recognizes this. The train of logic inevitably involves connecting a recent problem with data quality. Thus, a shipping manager may recognize that the large number of returned items is due to incorrect bills of lading, a chief financial officer may recognize that poor billing leads to higher-than-needed "bad debt," and the market planner may recognize that imprecise market share numbers impact the ability to plan the next ad campaign. Similarly, the chief information officer must explain that poor data quality has delayed a data warehousing effort. And the most senior executive becomes frustrated because two departments can't work together because "their numbers don't agree."

As consumers, people recognize poor quality data more readily. They are sensitive to billing errors, improperly addressed mail, and price claims on the Internet that turn out to be incorrect. Subtly in many cases, less subtly in others, consumers spend their dollars elsewhere (perhaps the most important, unknown statistic to most organizations is the "revenue lost due to customer dissatisfaction").

Organizations that have improved data quality and, importantly, sustained the gains report enormous benefit. They improve customer satisfaction, create empowered employees, and save enormous amounts of money. They make more confident decisions faster, and they can better align their departments.

This *Field Guide* aims to make the job a little easier. It consists of many short chapters, each as narrowly focused on a single topic as the author's skills permit. Read cover to cover, thirty-six chapters in eight sections address these questions that data quality leaders are likely to encounter:

- Who cares about data quality? Why worry about it?

- Does the business case hold up?

- What are the competing approaches and what will they get us?

- What is data anyway? And what is "data quality"?

- What technical methods are needed?

- What must middle managers do?

- What must senior managers do?

- What's next?

We do not expect many people to read *Data Quality: The Field Guide* cover to cover. We do recommend that everyone read Chapters 1, 7, 10, 15, and 33 (they take about 15 minutes to read and years to fully appreciate), then dive in to address the issues at hand. "Field tips" summarize the most important points of each chapter and are reorganized in Chapter 36. Many figures are of a "how-to" nature. These may be downloaded, in color, from the Butterworth-Heineman Web site (see "Instructions for Downloading Figures and Tables") and used in presentations, to stimulate discussions, and to align the organization. They may also be used "in the field" to evaluate a proposed data policy, to identify a social issue, to interpret a control chart, to move an improvement team along, to recall how an issue should be addressed, or in any of the hundreds of other ways that issue and opportunities pop up.

Most organizations, when they set their minds to it, can improve data quality levels by an order of magnitude or more. And the benefits are enormous. Good luck!

Author's Note

I've written two previous books, *Data Quality: Management and Technology* (Bantam, 1992) and *Data Quality for the Information Age* (Artech, 1996). My customers, some of them anyway, tell me that while they find the ideas, examples, and underlying theory useful, "they are just too academic."

On the one hand, no author likes to be criticized. I naturally think my explanations are poignant and lucid.

On the other hand, I firmly belief the adage "The best thing you can have is a demanding customer." So *Data Quality: The Field Guide* was written in response to the feedback, in the spirit of quality improvement.

I've tried to write *The Field Guide* so readers could skim most of it, study relevant sections, and consult specific "how-to's" as needed. I don't promise to have fully met the demands of the feedback. After all, improving data quality does require hard work (indeed, if having excellent data were easy, then all organizations would be enjoying the benefits). But I've done my best.

Let me know how you think I've done; please send your comments to *fieldguide@dataqualitysolutions.com*.

Acknowledgments

Despite the benefits of doing so, improving data quality is not easy. It may involve realigning responsibilities, getting to the root causes of errors and eliminating them, and making new kinds of measurements. Many changes involve working in new ways (not just harder) and so are quite threatening to people and organizations.

Perhaps because it is so hard, only the best people, those with the live heads, the strong backs, and the good hearts, lead data quality efforts. There are lots of these people out there and this *Field Guide* recognizes their contributions. I have been fortunate enough to work with dozens, maybe even hundreds of them, as colleagues or clients. And they have helped make this a better book.

I wish I could cite them, but many wish to remain anonymous. So here are their initials: PA, HA, MA, SA, BA, RA, RA, JA, PB, DB, BW, SB, TB, CB, BB, RB, CB, PB, JB, SB, SD, LB, MB, KB, MB, NB, FC, MC, PC, WC, MC, CC, CC, GC, MC, JC, CC, MD, AD, PD, KD, JD, SD, HD, PD, CD, AD, MD, PD, ND, CD, CE, LE, FE, DF, CF, BF, EF, BF, SF, BG, LG, PG, CG, NG, TG, SG, BG, RG, AG, JG, GG, BG, GG, GG, RG, JH, RH, HH, EH, GH, DH, GH, JH, YH, KI, JI, JJ, PJ, YJ, KJ, DJ, JJ, RK, RK, KK, MK, GK, BK, JK, JL, AL, AL, AL, CL, JL, DL, DL, JL, DL, KM, SM, AM, JM, SM, JM, BM, TM, SM, SM, MM, DM, DM, SM, KM, DN, MN, DN, TN, MN, JO, CO, VO, RP, MP, KP, BP, JP, CP, MP, PS, RP, PP, JR, AR, DR, DR, LR, BR, GS, PS, BS, KS, CS, NS, PS, GS, RS, MS, NS, JS, DS, CS, DS, PS, DS, AS, DT, ST, JT, LT, DT, AT, JT, ST, MT, AT, JT, JT, GU, RU, RW, AL, KW, PW, RW, JW, LW, DW, DW, SW, RW, RW, and JZ.

Thanks also to my co-workers at Navesink Consulting Group: Dennis Parton, Bob Pautke, Susan Stuntebeck, and Kathy Van Dam. Kathy Van Dam has reviewed and fixed up numerous drafts, and with good cheer! Their critical (I mean penetrating) insights have been most helpful. Thanks especially to Bob Pautke, my closest colleague for longer than he cares to remember and on whom I rely.

My family continues to become even more supportive. My brother-in-law, Frank Balkin, provides the perspective of a Hollywood agent. My father pushes me hard to be clear and succinct. My children, Jenn, Andy, and Greg, have really gotten into the "quality spirit" as they have grown older. They provide interesting examples and they are keen to give me a dose of my own medicine every time I make a mistake.

Last, my wife Nancy never ceases to amaze me. Not all "DQ days" are perfect. But she always is. She builds me up on the low days and builds me up still further on the good ones. The miracle that is us gets better every day.

Who Cares About Data Quality?

It turns out that almost everyone has a stake in data quality. Almost everyone, no matter what their job description, in any organization, large or small, public or private, brand new dot.com or old-style brick and mortar, is impacted by poor data. And probably, at least some of the time, almost everyone passes on poor data.

This section selects various perspectives—chief executive officers (Chapter 1), consumers and dot.coms (Chapter 2), chief financial officers and managers of ongoing operations (Chapter 3), marketers (Chapter 4), and chief information officers (Chapter 5) to describe some of the issues. Most chapters use specific types of data (Internet data, billing data, customer data, etc.) to make specific points. Each chapter points to the later chapters that describe resolution of the most important issues faced.

Chapter 6 is a catch-all chapter, just in case anyone feels left out.

Yes, Millie, Even CEOs Are Interested in Data Quality

Some think that no two words can cause a chief executive officer's eyes to glass over faster than "data quality" (and this applies to heads of government agencies, leaders of nonprofit organizations, etc.). "Data," aren't they the boring bits and bytes buried in our computer systems? And "quality," isn't the implication that our people aren't working hard enough?

Besides, people have real work to do, customers to satisfy, production schedules to meet, decisions to make, strategies to map out, a demanding board to answer. Who wants to worry about those bits and bytes when no one is complaining?

But CEOs are (or should be) passionately interested in data quality and for a wide variety of reasons.

First, bad data can earn the CEO and his or her organization a place in the national news and who needs that? The bombing of the Chinese Embassy is the most publicized recent example. But it happens more frequently than one might think. Further examples are described in Chapter 7.

Fortunately most cases of bad data do not land the organization or its leader on the front page. Unfortunately, poor quality data seems to be the norm. As CEOs know, the costs of poor quality data are enormous. Some costs, such as added expense and lost customers, are relatively easy to spot, if the organization looks. We suggest (based on a small number of careful, but proprietary studies), as a working figure, that these costs are roughly 10 percent of revenue for a typical organization. To date, no one, in hundreds of discussions, has suggested that this number is "way too high." CEOs naturally want to return these monies to the bottom line.

CEOs know that the 10 percent figure includes only the costs that are easy to measure. This figure does not include other costs, such as bad decisions and low morale, that are harder to measure but even more important.

CEOs are concerned about the havoc poor data can wreak on strategy. Every Information Age strategy, from exploiting the Internet, to globalization, supply chain management, knowledge management, and so forth depend on high-quality data. CEOs know they cannot set strategy without good data. And they know their organizations cannot execute without good data.

CEOs know superior quality data makes their companies stronger, more profitable, more flexible, and smarter.

They also know that, sooner or later, customers demand high quality. They've studied the penetration of quality management within the manufacturing sector to see that, in industry after industry, companies had three choices.

1.   They could lead the quality movement within their industry and earn higher profits.

2.   They could wait until their profits were threatened and try to catch up.

3.   They could be acquired.

Internet customers seem especially unforgiving of simple errors.

CEOs know that many companies are beginning to compete on the basis of superior data. Can there be any doubt that all information-based industries will be so impacted?

They also see the enormous market capitalizations awarded Information Age companies. They know that Information Age assets, including data, account for these valuations.

A few skeptics may remark that while data quality is certainly important, there are many others in the organization better suited to deal with it. After all, isn't data quality the CIO's (or CFO's) job? And, indeed, experience confirms that functional managers can improve data quality within their spans of control.

But CEOs know it is a risky proposition. They're aware that Joseph Juran, reflecting on the quality movement in manufacturing, remarked of their counterparts, "They thought they could make the right speeches, establish broad goals, and leave everything else to subordinates . . . They didn't realize that fixing quality meant fixing whole companies, a task that can't be delegated."[1]

---

1.   Joseph M. Juran, "Made in USA: A Renaissance in Quality," *Harvard Business Review* (July–August 1993):47.

CEOs know that data quality is even more demanding than manufacturing quality. Data cross organizational boundaries in the blink of the eye. And bad data are like viruses. There is simply no way of knowing where they will turn up or the damage they will cause. A seemingly mundane error in a customer order does not just cause a customer to complain. It slows revenue collection, leads to an error in inventory management and complicates financial accounting. Taken together, such errors cause decision makers to mistrust summary reports and proceed based on their intuition. Suppliers may be impacted. And on and on. And so on.

CEOs are especially concerned about social (read "political") issues (Chapters 33 and 34), organization (Chapter 32), and management roles (Chapters 30 and 31).

In short, CEOs are concerned about data quality because so much is at stake.

Field Tip 1.1: An organization's most senior leader must not delegate responsibility for data quality. The losses due to poor quality are simply too great. Fortunately, high-quality data earn enormous returns.

2

Internet Users Wonder, "Are These Prices Correct?" . . . and Dot.Coms Better Make Sure They Are

Sooner or later, consumers demand quality products and services. In the United States, consumers tend to tolerate quality problems when a product or service is "new." But over time they grow more demanding. People no longer accept, for example, a trip back to the dealer to fix their new car. And "quality" is a very personal concept—each consumer's needs are different than the needs of others. Over time, a few needs clarify themselves as most important to most people. "Safety" is a preeminent requirement of automobiles, for example.

The Internet is in its infancy as a means of doing business. The processes that clarify which user needs will be most important have only begun. Privacy is a good example. There are passionate views ranging from strict demands that data about Internet customers be guaranteed to the concept that privacy is old-fashioned.

This *Field Guide* recommends that consumers demand high quality data on the Internet. Not only will their immediate needs be met sooner, the processes of clarifying common needs will be hurried along.

What specifically should consumers demand? Each should define quality in his or her own terms and insist that the most important needs be met. The following list aims to help the consumer clearly articulate his or her needs. Items on the list are based on the most common needs of decision makers in large organizations (who have the most experience using data) and casual observation of what satisfies/annoys Internet users today. Internet consumers should insist that the Web-based organizations they do business with must, at the very least, address the following:

- How is "privacy" defined on this site, and how will their privacy be protected?

- What do the data and key terms mean? Does "lowest price" mean "lowest price anywhere guaranteed," or simply "lowest price on this Web site"?

- What may the data be used for and should they be interpreted? It may be fine that Web-site data are "suitable for use in a fourth-grader's history report" but not for serious commerce. And it may be fine that "every effort has been made to ensure that prices provided here are correct, but they are not guaranteed, so don't use them to plan your retirement." Whatever the intended use of data, the consumer has every right to know.

- Can the data be trusted? Are they accurate and up-to-date? Are all data published?

- What protection is provided if data prove wrong and I am harmed as a result?

- How do I get help?

Table 2.1 reformulates these questions and consumer demands in terms of the dimensions of data quality cited in Chapter 17.

Table 2.1   *Summary Expectations of the Data Consumer*

Category	Dimension	Data Consumer Expectation: The Data Consumer should expect . . .
Privacy	Consumer Privacy	that the Publisher will explicitly state and follow its consumer privacy policy.
	Privacy of Others	that the Publisher would explicitly state and follow its privacy policy regarding others, including other consumers, individuals, organizations, and so forth.
Content	Areas Covered	the Publisher to be explicit in describing what data are published and how they should used.
	Appropriate Use	the Publisher to describe appropriate and inappropriate uses of the published data.
	Comprehensiveness	that all data needed for an intended use are provided, unless otherwise stated.
	Definition	clear, easy-to-understand definitions of every important term, including measurement units.
	Original Source(s)	all original sources of data to be clearly stated.

Table 2.1 *Summary Expectations of the Data Consumer (continued)*

Category	Dimension	Data Consumer Expectation: The Data Consumer should expect . . .
Quality of Values	Accuracy	that all published data are correct and the Publisher will stand behind published data or state its policy regarding incorrect data.
	Currency	that data values are current, unless otherwise informed by the Publisher.
	Completeness	that all relevant data are published, unless otherwise informed by the Publisher.
	Formats	that data formats properly convey the data and are easy to read. Unless a format is straightforward, the Consumer should expect to find instructions on reading the data.
Presentation	Language	the Publisher's choice of language is clear and any technical terms used are fully defined.
	Ease of Interpretation	that if he/she follows instructions, he/she will properly interpret data.
Improvement	Feedback	that he/she has a means to convey his/her comments about data, good or bad, to the Publisher and that these comments will be acted upon in a responsible manner.
	Measurement	to be provided useful summaries of actual quality levels of the data he/she is using and to be notified if recently published data are abnormally deficient.
	Track Record	a summary of performance measurements indicating the results of improvements.
Commitment	Help	that he/she can easily ask and have answered any questions regarding the proper use or meaning of data, update schedules, etc.
	Commitment	that the Publisher is fair and honest and will provide him/her the benefit of any doubt. The Consumer also should expect the Publisher to adhere to its published policies.

Now consider data quality from the point of view of the dot.com (or the dot.com department of a larger organization). Again, though the Internet is in its infancy, a few points regarding data quality and the Internet are clear from this point of view. The first is that data organizations have heretofore maintained as proprietary are now available to the general public. One of the brutal realities of data quality is that the quality needs of different customers, even inside the organization, are so diverse. The Internet will surely exacerbate this issue. The number of data customers will increase dramatically, and the ways they use the data may be very different. Their backgrounds will be diverse, and consumers cannot be trained on the nuances of data the way employees can be trained. This point is true for business-to-business uses of the Internet as well, though perhaps to a lesser extent for those organizations that are integrating their supply chains.

The second point is that naïve consumers may be more easily victimized by bad data. They simply do not have the background necessary to recognize data values that cannot possibly be correct. Nor can they be expected to understand technical terms or code sets used every day within the organization.

Third, dot.coms, as with all organizations, need to adopt strategies that distinguish themselves from others. Higher quality data is one means of doing this. Sooner or later their competitors will. The first will achieve a measure of advantage. This advantage may prove decisive—after all, most consumers want to trust the companies they do business with. And since there is so little face-to-face interaction, there are fewer ways for dot.coms to earn that trust. Competitive advantages seem especially important in Internet time.

At the very least, consumers will find it difficult to trust organizations whose data consistently prove to be of low quality. As data quality leaders gain advantage, other dot.coms may find themselves forced to improve, or lose business. The pattern in which quality is first adapted by a few leaders to gain advantage and then copied by others to catch up, has played out in any number of industries.

The methods presented herein are directly applicable to data published on the Internet. First, a dot.com can (and should) conduct customer needs analyses to understand data consumers' expectations (Chapter 17). To date, the quality issue of greatest importance seems to be privacy. While issues of privacy may take decades to sort out, responsible organizations can at least publish and adhere to Web privacy policies. Many are doing so.

Second, a dot.com can and should provide simple statements about quality levels, protection, and so forth (Chapter 18). A few Web sites do this now, even if the statement is no more than "accuracy of these data cannot be guaranteed and XYX organization makes no guarantee as to their quality."

Third, the dot.com can make needed improvements, based on gaps between customer needs and measured quality levels (Chapter 22). It will probably be particularly important that simple "data dictionaries" explaining key terms, units of measurement (e.g., are these U.S. dollars or Australian dollars?), and so on be prominently displayed.

Fourth, the dot.com should solicit and act on consumer feedback.

Table 2.2 recasts Table 2.1 from the perspective of the dot.com and describes appropriate actions to satisfy consumer needs.

Table 2.2   *Summary Guidelines for the Data Publisher*

Category	Dimension	Data Publisher Guideline: The Data Publisher should . . .
Privacy	Consumer Privacy	develop, publish, and adhere to its privacy policy. A simply stated and applied policy is preferred. Obviously the policy must adhere to all applicable laws.
	Privacy of Others	develop, state, and adhere to its overall privacy policy. A simply stated and applied policy is preferred. Obviously the policy must adhere to all applicable laws. The policy should cover any individual, organization, or other entity about which data are gathered and/or published.
Content	Areas Covered	describe what data are available at the Web site and how they should be used.
	Appropriate Use	provide explicit descriptions and possibly examples of the appropriate use(s) of the data they are providing. Likewise, specific ways in which the data should not be used should be identified.
	Comprehensiveness	ensure that all data needed to complete each intended use are provided. If needed data are not provided, the Publisher should clearly state this and, if possible, advise the Consumer where those data may be obtained.
	Definition	clearly define each data element, attribute, and measurement unit. The Publisher should make it easy for the Consumer to find and use these definitions.
	Original Sources	clearly define the original source(s) of all data, including sources from within the Publisher's organization and the sources of data obtained from third parties.

Table 2.2   *Summary Guidelines for the Data Publisher (continued)*

Category	Dimension	Data Publisher Guideline: The Data Publisher should . . .
Quality of Values	Accuracy	provide the most accurate data possible. If data are not 100% correct, publish a measurement of the accuracy level. The Publisher should clearly state its policy regarding incorrect data.
	Currency	keep data current at all times. If this is not possible, the Publisher should clearly state the date and time at which values were current. The Publisher should stand behind values that are no longer current or clearly articulate its policy regarding values that are no longer current.
	Completeness	publish all relevant data. If this is not possible or desired, the Publisher should clearly state what is not published. If possible, the Publisher should advise the Consumer how he/she may obtain the missing data.
Presentation	Formats	carefully choose formats for presenting data. Avoid dense tables and complicated graphs and explain technical terms.
	Language	use the language of its intended audience. Ideally, if large numbers of Consumers require a second (third . . .) language, the Publisher should have separate sites in the second (third . . .) language.
	Ease of Interpretation	make data as easy to interpret as possible. If there is any chance of misinterpretation, the Publisher should provide easy-to-follow instructions.
Improvement	Feedback	provide mechanisms by which the Consumer can provide feedback. Analyze comments to identify opportunities for improvement and take appropriate action.
	Measurement	develop measurement capabilities that provide detailed results of actual quality levels. Provide timely summaries to the Data Consumer. Identify "out-of-control" situations and inform the Consumer.
	Track Record	provide a usable set of results that accurately provide a historical view of their performance results. Act on feedback and measurements, identify root causes of errors, and mitigate them.

Table 2.2 *Summary Guidelines for the Data Publisher (continued)*

Category	Dimension	Data Publisher Guideline: The Data Publisher should . . .
Commitment	Help	provide a variety of help capabilities. At a minimum, this should include prompt replies to mailed questions. If possible, questions should be answered in real time.
	Commitment	make its commitment to the Consumer as clear as possible. At the very least, provide its policies regarding published data to the Data Consumer and adhere to them.

© Data Laboratories, LLP. Used with permission. Downloaded from datalaboratories.com.

DISCLAIMER: Data Laboratories, LLC provides consumers of data and publishers of data with a structure and criteria for the exchange of information that occurs during the presentation of data and the subsequent consumption of data. Data Laboratories, LLC does not certify the quality of underlying data. ALL WARRANTIES OF MERCHANTABILITY AND FITNESS FOR ANY PARTICULAR PURPOSE WHETHER EXPRESSED OR IMPLIED ARE HEREBY DISCLAIMED TO THE FULL EXTENT PERMITTED BY APPLICABLE LAW.

Field Tip 2.1: The Internet is virgin territory for data quality. Dot.coms will need to establish trust with consumers. Those that provide high-quality data have a better chance of doing so and can expect to achieve competitive advantages. Those who don't may be at a disadvantage.

3

Chief Financial Officers and Managers of Ongoing Operations Need to Know "Where the Money Is"

Chief financial officers care about data quality because all their knowledge about the organization's assets and liabilities stems from data. Indeed, in most organizations relatively little cash actually changes hands—transactions are nothing more than data flying back and forth.

Distinctions between line and staff jobs aside, operational managers care about data quality for much the same reason—the only way they know about what they manage is through data. A lot of inventory management is knowing "how many there are." This is also true for many operational processes. Operational processes themselves both create and use huge amounts of data.

This chapter considers "billing" both as a specific instance of data (and an information chain) that most organizations can well stand to improve and as an example to illustrate the more general points for similar data (and information chains).

Obviously, most organizations are both creators and recipients of invoices, though different departments are involved. Business units (or divisions) are "billers" (i.e., they invoice their customers for products and services provided) and accounts payable (or its equivalent) receives invoices from suppliers and pays them. These departments may have different perspectives on billing based on their respective roles.

Essentially, however, there are only two important billing issues: overbilling, in which the customer is billed more than he or she should be, and underbilling, in which the customer is billed less. Importantly, the overbilling issue receives the most attention. In particular, many (most/all) customers review the invoices they receive and complain about overbilling. And the biller, in most cases, has a large customer service department to answer billing questions, make adjustments, and so forth. Some organizations keep reasonable track of how much revenue they rebate in this way (we some-

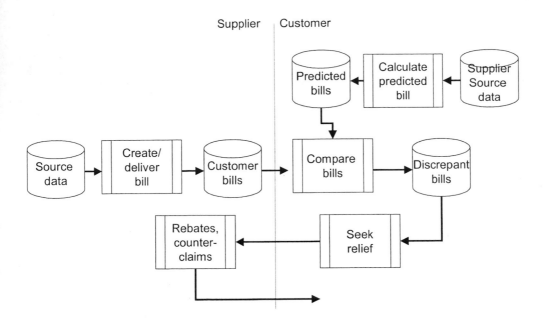

Figure 3.1   *Typical quality system for customer billing*

times hear that "one percent of revenue" is typical). They may also know
the cost of this error detection and correction. In large organizations,
accounts payable may also track how much time and expense it incurs to
find errors and seek corrections. Both the organization supplying the bill
and the organization receiving it bear added costs. Neither can "close the
books" promptly. And contention over billing does nothing to advance
their relationship. In toto, the quality system is as depicted in Figure 3.1.
(The data quality aficionado is usually repulsed by inspection and rework
that involves the customer.)

Few customers report underbilling, and most organizations have no way
of knowing the extent of this issue. But, if an organization overbills, it must:

- Underbill by about the same amount (or more), or

- Systematically overbill, a possibly fraudulent act.

A billing system is "unbiased" if the total amounts of overbilling and
underbilling are about the same. A billing system is "biased toward overbilling" if it systematically overbills by more than it underbills and "biased
toward underbilling" if it systematically underbills. Assume that the billing
system was unbiased some time in the past. Since many overbilling issues

have been reported, it is possible that the root causes of some have been eliminated. If so, there is currently more underbilling than overbilling (and the billing system is biased toward underbilling).

In terms of the customer-supplier model (discussed in Chapter 16), while the feedback channel for overbilling is usually pretty effective, it is nonexistent for underbilling.

To illustrate the overall impact, assume the following:

	Cost to Biller
Value-added cost to create an invoice	1% of revenue
Non–value-added cost to correct errors	1% of revenue
Cost of underbilling	1% of revenue
Added cost of ill will	unknown
Added cost incurred because books cannot be closed, etc.	unknown

It is evident that the "cost of poor data quality" is at least two percent of revenue, for a simple information chain whose "value-added costs" are only one percent of revenue. Expressed as a percentage, the cost of poor data quality for billing is 200 percent. A similar calculation can be constructed by accounts payable.

Billers should apply information chain management (Chapter 27) and accounts payable should apply supplier management (Chapter 26) to recover much of this cost. Experience confirms that roughly 70 percent of the total costs of poor data quality can be recovered.

From the customer's perspective, the quality system shown in Figure 3.1 is simply untenable. Supplier management can replace it with the system shown in Figure 3.2.

From the biller's perspective, the billing chain is not as simple as it may appear. It involves numerous hand-offs of data, the result of normal business activity, including value-added activities (see Figure 3.3) such as the following:

- Marketing, which yields new customers and pricing schemes

- Sales, which yield customer purchases

- New product developments, which yield new products

- Customer payments

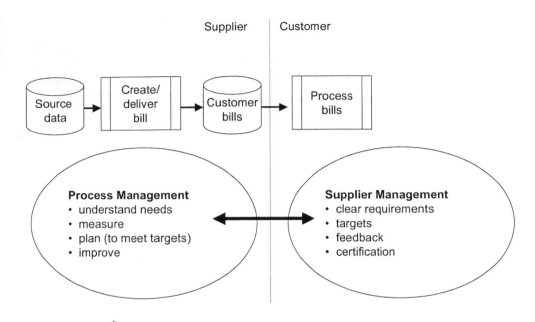

Figure 3.2   *Desired quality system for billing*

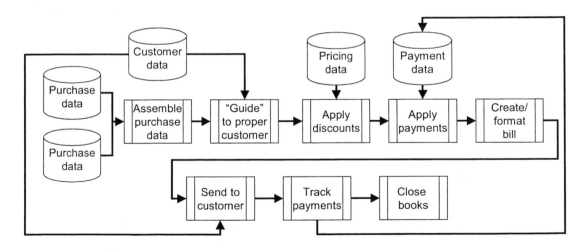

Figure 3.3   *A billing chain involves many hand-offs*

Billing issues occur not because the billers or those upstream are inept, but rather because so many hand-offs in the end-to-end billing chain are unmanaged. Process management is strikingly effective because it addresses these weaknesses.

A second-best, but still effective approach involves billers treating (internal) departments that supply data needed for billing as they would external suppliers.

Field Tip 3.1: Look for opportunities to improve data quality "where the money is." Billing is a natural. Many organizations find that they can reduce underbilling for little added cost.

4

Marketers Need to Know about Their Customers

Marketing managers care about data quality because data capture almost everything they know about customers, the marketplace, competitors, and practically everything else. The rare exceptions might be some technical details that salespeople keep to themselves. A salesperson may know, for example, that a box of fine Cuban cigars is needed to secure final approval from a particular customer. Pertinent though such details may be, they are usually kept private.

This chapter uses customer data in four ways.

1. As a specific instance of data that most organizations should improve.

2. To illustrate the connection between quality data and business strategy.

3. To illustrate to marketing managers more general concerns about data quality.

4. As a timely instance of a particularly difficult issue—namely, promulgating standard definitions of key terms.

Before digging into details, it is important to recognize that there are three possible definitions of the term "customer data."

1. Data that directly impact the customer—billing data fit this definition and are the subject of Chapter 3.

2. Data that customers see—billing data and data published on the Internet both fit this definition. Internet data are the subject of Chapter 2.

3. Data about customers—whoever accesses and uses them—these data are the subject of this chapter.

While customer data are important to all organizations, they are especially important to organizations pursuing a strategy of "customer intimacy." An important result described by Michael Treacy and Fred Wiersma is that leading companies, consciously or not, pursue one of three strategies: customer intimacy, product leadership, or price leadership. It seems evident that an organization's most important data are those that it requires (or those that enable it) to implement strategy. Customer data are clearly critical to organizations pursuing customer intimacy. An oft-repeated anecdote involves the business unit of one company whose sole focus was on the top 90 customers (individuals). It seems evident that this business unit's goal was to be customer-intimate. But its databases did not reliably indicate whether customers were male or female. We claim that it is extremely difficult to become intimate with a person when you don't know if "he" is a man or a woman.

Customer data are also important to organizations pursuing other strategies. For product leaders, the goal is to develop and bring to market more innovative products faster, so it would seem that design, engineering, and manufacturing data would be more important. But this is not necessarily so. Product leaders must also know which customers buy leading-edge products. And they must have intimate knowledge about how these customers use the "latest and greatest." So at least some customer data are critical.

Price leaders face the challenge of reducing unit costs in everything they do. They can't afford to bear the added costs of finding and fixing simple errors. Billing data are of great interest. And some other customer data may be as well.

Note that the specifics of their interests may be different. The price leader needs the basic facts: customer ID, products ordered, payment history, address, and so on. The product leader is not equally interested in every customer. But he or she needs to understand the leading-edge customers in great detail. Indeed, as leading-edge products become "smarter," details regarding how these products are used and "fit in" become even more critical.

Companies pursuing customer intimacy face two common problems. First, they want to develop a common definition so the various business units can all work from a "common view of the customer." Second, customer databases are plagued by errors.

The second problem is relatively straightforward, and consistent application of the techniques described in sections E (customer needs analysis, measurement, control, improvement, and planning), F (information chain and supplier management), and G (senior leadership, policy, and culture) work well. The interface between the sales department (and sometimes individual salespeople) and the rest of the organization is a frequent source of poor data quality and must be addressed.

One frequently cited issue (whether the organization is customer-intimate or not) is the high return rate of direct mail. Upward of 20 percent of direct mail is undeliverable and a frequent complaint is that the data supplied by the "mailing list company" are of poor quality. There are other problems as well. Two are misspelled names for mail that is delivered and duplicate mailings. Data supplier management can help increase the accuracy of these data and other data purchased from external sources (supplier management is helpful even if the data received from outside sources are obtained for free). At the same time, organizations trying to become intimate with customers must develop their own unique sources.

The issues associated with developing a common definition of customer and getting business units to work from a common and complete view of the customer are very difficult. Not only is it technically difficult to pull off, the social issues are wicked. Business units seem to cover their customers and are simply unwilling to share data about them (issues of data ownership are discussed in Chapter 31). Business units tend to distrust the hype that "we'll be able to cross-sell" or "create new efficiencies in dealing with customers." Those leading the charge to create a common definition, often from marketing or headquarters, point out that customers don't want to have to deal with multiple business units to conduct business. But they are often insensitive to the bottom-line results that business units must achieve. Figure 4.1 summarizes the pros and cons of the common definition. But the positions are irreconcilable, and damaging political battles are inevitable.

At the root of the issue is the failure to consider diverse (data) customer needs. On the one hand, those promoting a common view have one set of needs. On the other, individual business units have, over the years, aligned their data model to suit their approach to customers. The two sets of needs are different, and one database cannot possibly meet them.

Once people recognize that "the other side's" needs are legitimate, many possible solutions present themselves. This statement assumes the relationships that the various business units have with customers are acceptable. But if the real issue is "We want to conduct business differently," the solution proposed will not work. The heart of one such solution is a "customer index." The index is nothing more than a cross-reference giving each customer a master identifier, indicating which business unit databases also contain data on that customer, and providing the primary keys needed to

Pros	Cons
• Many customers expect companies to treat them in an integrated way.	• Each business unit has defined "customer" in the way best suited to its business. Many of the differences are virtually irreconcilable.
• A single customer care center can lead to cost savings.	• Business units are naturally skeptical of initiatives from "headquarters."
• Compelling opportunities to cross-sell	• Most business units want some means to hear from customers directly.
• The intangible benefits of common definitions across the company	• Most business units don't want to change, especially if all is working well.

Figure 4.1   *Common definition of customer*

identify that customer in those databases (see Table 4.1 for an example). In simple circumstances, where a business unit must conduct a simple transaction with a customer, it need not create or access a common view. If a customer has a simple question regarding another business unit, the business unit can find the required data easily. More complex questions, such as may

Table 4.1   *Examples of Data in a Customer Index*

Common Identifiers	Common Name	John A. Smith	John B. Smith	Jon Smith	
	Index Number	123456789	234567890	345678901	
	Business units with data about this customer	A, B, C	A, B	B	
Business Unit A Identifiers	Name	J. A. Smith	J. B. Smith		And so on for all customers
	Key	JAS-7	JBS-2		
Business Unit B Identifiers	Name	John Smith	John Smith	J. Smith	
	Key	27-BC-Smith	13-AB-Smith	193-J-Smith	
Business Unit C Identifiers	Name	Smith, J.	Not Applicable		
	Key	SmithJ123	Not Applicable		
And so on for all business units					

be posed by the marketing department as it plans its next campaign, can also be satisfied.

We wish to emphasize that while solutions such as the one described above are feasible, they are not easy to implement. The data council (Chapter 30) should be directly accountable for such projects.

Field Tip 4.1. The most important data are those required for executing the most important strategies.

Field Tip 4.2: Business units arrive at different definitions of "customer" because they run their businesses differently.

Field Tip 4.3: Getting business units to agree on a common definition is almost impossible. Recognize legitimate business needs and develop data structures to meet them.

5

Chief Information Officers Are Stuck in the Middle

A Chief Information Officer is almost always worried about data quality. For him or her, the situation is more involved and subtle than for others. If financial data are wrong, the Chief Financial Officer feels immediate pain. And if the organization can't agree on a common definition of "customer," the marketing manager feels the pain. A CIO's uses of data do not have direct impact on Profit and Loss, so they don't feel the pain in the same immediate ways.[1]

The CIO's worries about data quality stems from people's immediate reaction that she must be to blame if the data are not perfect. Indeed, at first glance many people conclude that "If it's in the computer, it must be right." If the data are not right, they naturally conclude that the problem lies with the computer, and so must be the CIO's responsibility.

A second reason that CIOs concern themselves with data quality is their departments spend (some say "waste") an inordinate amount of time and effort[2] dealing with poor quality data. They:

- "Clean-up" bad data when they implement a new system so the bad data will not compromise user acceptance.

- Write software so that systems can "talk to each other."

- Develop and implement technologies to support new business initiatives such as "customer resource management," data mining, and enterprise systems.

- Respond to user questions about "what the data mean."

Organizations in general and CIOs in particular ignore this point at their peril. There is a critical shortage of qualified IT personnel. The best

---

1. CIOs will, of course, point out that they feel lots of pain stemming from immediate sources.
2. Estimates of the percentage of a typical IT department's budget that is devoted to data quality range up to 50 percent.

technologists ought to be building infrastructure to support the future, not cleaning up mundane data errors.

A third reason that CIOs worry about data quality is that they are responsible for at least some important data. This chapter uses data resource data and data warehouses as two specific examples of such data. And, as with other examples throughout this book, the examples illustrate general issues the CIO must resolve.

At the same time, there are many data quality issues that the CIO is uniquely unqualified to solve. Consider the billing chain of Chapter 3. If that chain is broken (say one root cause of error is that the needed data from the Sales Department are not supplied to the billing chain on time. Deeper still, there could be animosity between the two departments), and no technological wizardry can resolve the issue.

5.1   Data resource data

An extremely important and often ignored category of data is *data resource data*. Data resource data are data that describe the data resource. It includes definitions of terms (attributes, fields etc.) such as CUSTOMER, and much more, as explained below. They are more commonly called "metadata" (data about data). In most organizations, the IT department is intimately involved in the creation or acquisition of data resource data. It (the IT department) creates data resource data when it defines new databases and builds new systems. IT also acquires data resource data when it purchases systems from software vendors.

At their most basic level, data resource data describe data models. Thus they define what terms (entities and attributes) mean in (hopefully) simple business language. For example, definitions of the entity "sale" and all attributes about that sale—customer name, customer address, purchased items, price, delivery date, and so forth are all provided by the data resource data. The most important customers of these definitions are usually data customers who use these definitions to properly interpret and use data.

Data resource data should also answer simple questions that data customers may be expected to ask, including:

- How do I gain access?
- What are the original sources of these data?
- Are there limitations on the uses of these data?

- How do I get help?

- What must I do to get the data model changed and/or extended?

Even something as basic as the name given to a data field is data resource data. Confusing names may cause users of a system to misinterpret them.

Importantly, developers are also customers of data resource data and they require much deeper information. For example, the database developer must know how attributes are related to one another to construct the actual database and the application developer must know how to fetch data so they can be presented to data customers. Naturally, these needs are very different than the needs of other (business) data customers.

At a somewhat higher level, the entire organization is a customer for data resource data.[3] Entities and attributes are usually included in more than one database. A data customer that wishes to integrate data from multiple databases may be misled if the definitions of common entities and attributes are different. Thus the term "customer" may mean one thing in one database and something slightly different in another.

This example underscores the importance of standards or conventions. One such convention involves the names given each entity and attribute as part of the data modeling process. Ideally, if entities in two data structures mean the same thing, they are given the same name and if they mean something different, even subtly so, they should be given different names.

One other important question is the ability to find needed data. As it stands today, in most organizations a potential data customer who asks, "Do we have any data about xyz?" is left to her personal network to find the answer.

The public library offers a simple model of good practice. Consider just "books" and the question "What books are available on such and such a subject?" In most communities, a person need only visit the public library to get a good answer and obtain several pertinent books. The library provides a number of "information agents" to assist, including card catalogs and research librarians. Books not immediately available may usually be obtained via interlibrary loans. A final component involves developing and keeping the card catalog current. Though there are hundreds of publishers, a simple process owned by the Library of Congress is quite effective.

---

3.   Understanding customer needs is more difficult, though not insurmountable, when the customer is an abstraction as opposed to a real, live person.

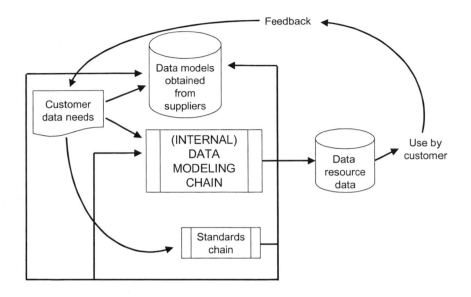

Figure 5.1   *Data resource data chain*

In most organizations, the data resource data are not up to the standards suggested by the library. For data obtained from the outside, supplier management (Chapter 26) should extend to data resource data as well. And internally, apply information chain management (Chapter 27) to implement a high-level data resource data chain. As Figure 5.1 depicts, two other information chains supply the data resource chain, a data modeling chain for systems analysts and other data modelers to follow and standards chains to provide needed conventions.

5.2   Data warehouses

Poor data quality can stymie successful implementation of a data warehouse (just as it can stymie a reengineering project—see Chapter 25). The key idea of course, is to build data quality into the warehouse, rather than worrying about it after implementation.[4] Like (almost) all data quality efforts, doing so is multifaceted and requires up-front planning.

---

4.   This *Field Guide* stresses the position that building data quality into a data warehouse is not really the right way of thinking at all. That mode of thought places technology, rather than customer needs, at the core. A better way to approach the problem is to first understand customer needs. There may well be needs that cannot be met by existing information chains and technologies. For example, an organization may not be able to "create a full picture of all the business we do with customers" because the relevant data are stored in operational systems owned by individual business units. A data warehouse may be technical means of choice to do so. But the need is not to "implement a data warehouse." It is to "solve a specified business problem" or "create an opportunity," and the project should be titled as such.

The data quality job is much more difficult if the CIO must pursue it alone. Further, the technological challenges in implementing a data warehouse: selecting and implementing the best systems, getting the data from source systems to the warehouse, and transforming and integrating data into the warehouse, are steep enough for most IT departments without the added burden of data quality. Tools vendors may not be all that helpful either, taking the narrow view that the essential data quality issue involves cleaning up source data (for which they provide tools[5]).

Issues associated with assigning data responsibilities to IT aside, there are some rather more basic reasons that building data quality into a data warehouse is challenging:

- There are different customers for data warehouses than for operational systems and they, quite naturally, have different quality requirements.

- The underlying decision-making chains (Chapter 28) may be more poorly understood than operational processes. This further complicates the understanding of customer needs.

- In operational systems, new data tend to be far more important. But the customer needs that give rise to data warehouses may involve the "historical record." New data are still critical, but older data are important as well.

- Many warehouses draw data from numerous operational sources. Warehouse customers require that names, formats, code sets, and so forth be standardized. And most organizations have no processes for doing so. As discussed in Chapter 32, standardization can be a notoriously difficult political issue.

- Even if the organization manages to successfully clean up data upon entry into the warehouse, doing so on a day-in and day-out basis proves to be a daunting challenge.

The techniques presented in this *Field Guide* apply well to data warehousing. Specifically, the CIO must:

- Separate data issues from more traditional technical issues and assign lead responsibility for data to someone within the customer community. As described below, this person's job is that of a data supplier manager, and we call this person the "warehouse supplier manager."

---

5.   This statement is not meant to castigate tools vendors. As explained later in Chapter 29, clean-up tools, properly focused and applied, can play an important role.

- As with all quality efforts, the warehouse supplier manager's first step must be to understand customer needs on an ongoing basis.

- Next the warehouse supplier manager deploys customer needs and quality requirements to appropriate sources or suppliers. For example, she may decide that legacy systems A, B, and C are needed to meet a completeness requirement (i.e., all customer data), that data names should be developed via a planning project led by customers, and that a measurement tool should be built into the data transformation tool to be supplied by IT.

- It is essential that data sources be brought up to spec, before the initial implementation of the data warehouse. This may require one or more iterations of measurement and improvement conducted at the source. As an example "Date-of-Birth" may have been an optional field within an operational system, but data warehouse customers need to know "a customer's age, give or take a year."

  Getting sources to agree to meet new requirements can be a daunting challenge. Source organizations may already have too much to do. They may be ambivalent about, even opposed to, the warehousing project. And so they can stymie the effort. Either party (the warehouse supplier manager or the source organization) must be able to turn to the data council for resolution.[6]

- Finally, already existing data must be brought up to spec. Here is where data clean-up tools may be profitably employed. They are focused specifically on historical data. And, applied this way they satisfy rule 4 of Chapter 13 (never employ a clean-up tool twice).

5.3   A trap and an opportunity

The superior way to improve data quality is at the source(s) of the data. If the CIO is the source, he should accept, even demand accountability. Data resource data meets this criterion. So does the task of migrating and translating data from operational systems to data warehouses.

Conversely, if the CIO is not the source of data, he must not take responsibility for quality. Almost all financial data, customer data, and other data created day-in and day-out by the business meet this criteria.

---

6.   This point illustrates why representation on the data council (Chapter 30) must be so broad.

The CIO must accept responsibility to automate well-defined and managed information chains. Supporting technologies must promote data quality.

The trap is that the CIO accepts responsibility for things he cannot possibly control. The CIO should not, for example take responsibility for cleaning up operational data that are created in error.

The opportunity is to provide leadership. Thus the CIO may be uniquely positioned to lead a data council (Chapter 30) and to help fix management accountabilities for data quality where they belong, across the entire organization. Finally, the CIO can lead efforts on standards. This *Field Guide* has cited several instances of departments interpreting common terms, such as "customer" or "sale" differently. The organization must agree on "standards." And the CIO is a good choice to own the standards information chain.

Standards are tricky. When they are well defined and implemented, they improve communications throughout. When poorly defined and/or implemented, they are ignored. And certain terms should not be standardized. Thus the sales and legal departments may have perfectly valid business reasons to define "sale" differently. The term should not be standardized.

Field Tip 5.1: Insist that data suppliers provide and keep data resource data current.

Field Tip 5.2: Implement an end-to-end *data resource chain* to ensure that data resource data are well-defined, kept up-to-date, and made easily available to all. Implement *data modeling* and *standards chains* as support.

Field Tip 5.3: Begin, not by cleaning up inadequate data resource data, but by implementing the data resource chain.

Field Tip 5.4: Build data quality into a data warehouse. One way to do so is name a warehouse supplier manager, who functions much like any other data supplier manager.

Field Tip 5.5: Allow ample time for data quality up-front in the warehouse effort. Warehouse customers and their needs are new and meeting them requires many sources to do their parts.

6

Just in Case You Didn't See Yourself in Chapters 1–5

If you feel relieved that you don't have to worry about data quality because you weren't named in Chapters 1–5, then you've made a grievous mistake. The only people who need not worry about data quality are those who neither create nor use data. No one participating in any modern economy can make that claim. Just to be clear, here are further examples and some generalizations. Everyone should identify with one or more of these scenarios.

First, everyone is a consumer. Even if you're not doing business via the Internet, others have data about you. At the very least, your credit report data are of great interest. Other businesses and agencies use data about you to sell you products and services. Much data are bad. Measure the height of a stack of a week's mail that is improperly addressed if you don't believe it. And of course you depend on data about their products (price, features, delivery data, etc.) to make purchase decisions.

General managers of large organizations (either companies or government agencies) will identify most closely with CEOs (Chapter 1). Similarly, those who own or work for small companies or start-ups (dot.coms especially) identify with everyone because they wear all hats at some time or another. Some data may be more critical for creating revenue—other data are simply for managing the store.

Those with staff jobs (human resources, knowledge management, facilities planning) will identify with chief financial officers and marketers. The data most important to them are not customer data but the data needed to support their functions (employee data, experts data, facilities data).

Middle managers in line organizations usually think they have the toughest jobs (and many of them are right). They identify with all of the worst problems throughout Chapters 1–5.

The impact of poor data quality on the customer service department was discussed in Chapter 3 (billing). Those who interact directly with customers also (salespeople, delivery people, etc.) identify with the problems cited in Chapter 4.

Decision makers and planners are highly dependent on data and thus care about data quality. They almost always depend on "facts" on which to base their decisions. There are, of course, plenty of exceptions. Many managers have operated from the seats of their pants their entire careers and don't want to be confused with the facts.

People who do "real work," whether it is operating a machine, loading delivery vehicles, or entering customer data, are part of larger business processes that both use data supplied by others and create new data. The billing chain example is directly relevant.

As with marketers and chief financial officers, decision makers and planners are dependent on data to make good decisions. While almost by definition decision making involves uncertainty, decision makers and planners want to base their decisions and plans on data they can trust.

No industry is immune. The data go by different names in the various industries. Hospitals refer to customers as patients, consultants as clients, software producers as users, brokers as accounts, and so forth. But all are customers, and the data about them are customer data.

Data quality is especially important to people in public service. Not only are the day-in and day-out jobs highly dependent on data, the public and funders demand results. These customers want to see what they're getting for their money. They expect agencies to self-report, and they need to trust these reports.

Field Tip 6.1: Everyone who either uses or creates data must be concerned about data quality. No one is left out. No one in any industry or government. No one at any level of management. No job category. And the impact of data quality is just as great in private life.

The Business Case for Data Quality

This section consists of three chapters designed to help leaders build a business case for data quality. While poor data quality and its impact makes the national and business news from time to time (Chapter 7), most data quality issues are buried deep within the organization (Chapter 8). They sap an organization's strength. They make it more difficult to satisfy customers, cost time and money, and compromise decision making. They make it more difficult to do the things the organization wants to do.

All of these points were made, by example, in Chapters 1–6. Chapters 7 and 8 summarize them in a way that makes building the business case easier. They comprise a "laundry list" of the issues.

The best way to get others in the organization interested is to call out the impact of poor data on the organization's most important strategies (Chapter 9).

Disasters Played Out in Public

Though national newspapers do not have sections entitled "Those Who Fail to Deliver Good Data," bad data and their impact make the national news regularly. The most infamous recent case was the bombing of the Chinese Embassy during the Kosovo war. The error made headlines for days and was still newsworthy months later when Secretary Cohen visited China to apologize on behalf of the United States. Follow-up commentary examined the incident from all angles.

According to a *New York Times* summary,[1] the most pertinent story line is as follows:

- The United States and allies undertook an air campaign to drive Serbs from Kosovo in June thru July 1999.

- Many government agencies recommended targets for bombing by the United States Air Force.

- The CIA picked one such target, thought to be an armory for Yugoslav weapons.

- The target was located using an out-of-date address. Instead of the armory, the building at the address now housed the Chinese Embassy.

- A usually-effective target review process failed to catch the error. In particular, one analyst who harbored suspicions of the target was away from the office at a critical time.

- The bomb hit the building it was targeted for, destroying Chinese Embassy, killing three Chinese Nationals and wounding 20.

- Though the United States admitted its error, the Chinese government was suspicious. Eventually the United States paid $28M compensation to the Chinese government.

1.   Steven Lee Meyers, "C.I.A. Fires Officer Blamed in Bombing of Chinese Embassy," *The New York Times*, April 9, 2000, p. A1.

Quite evidently most of the time a bit of bad data does not have such horrific impact, but the example illustrates a number of points about data quality:

- First, the real problem (the failure to note the correct addresses of the intended target and the Chinese Embassy) occurred far upstream of the damage.

- Second, errors are hard to correct.

- Third, this was not the only time the United States mistargeted a weapon. It happens more frequently than one might hope.[2] Fortunately, many times the impact is small. The bad news is that the impact (and the related cost) is unpredictable.

- The true "total cost of data poor quality" is incalculable.

Organizations that think they can't land in the national news for bad data because they do not drop bombs should not feel smug. It can happen in almost any industry.

The health industry has been rocked with the news that poor quality kills up to 98,000 people annually.[3] Fortunately, not all these deaths are due to poor data, but many are. Poor prescriptions are a good example.

The travel industry has enough problems with customer satisfaction without complaints that monitors displaying flight data are incorrect.[4]

One wonders if the EPA can lead the charge to clean up the environment if it cannot find the dumps.[5]

And all companies can be embarrassed by incorrect earnings reports. It happened 364 times in 1997–1999[6]—at least three cases grabbed headlines in 1999 alone.[7]

---

2. Edward Coy, "Under Iraqi Skies, A Canvas of Death," *The Washington Post*, 6/16/00, p. 1.
3. Robert Pear, "Group Asking U.S. for New Vigilance in Patient Safety," *The New York Times*, November 30, 1999, National Desk.
4. Adam Bryant, "Why Flying is So Awful," *Newsweek*, July 10, 2000, p. 38.
5. Melody Peterson, "Cleaning Up in the Dark; Companies Disclose Little About Costs of Toxic Sites," *The New York Times*, May 14, 1998, Business/Financial Desk.
6. "Accounting Wars," *Business Week*, September 25, 2000, p. 158.
7. "Rite Aid Calls Earnings Forecast Inaccurate," *The New York Times*, November 11, 1999, p. Cl.
    "McKesson To Restate Earnings for Four Quarters and Stock Falls 48%," *The New York Times*, April 29, 1999, Business Financial Desk.
    Gretchen Morgenson – Market Watch, "Oh, Those Pesky Little Financial Details," *The New York Times*, January 31, 1999.

Amazon.com is changing an entire industry (maybe even every industry), but they gain no benefit by publishing incorrect prices.[8] Toys R Us didn't enhance their reputation by not delivering the correct merchandise on the promised date.[9]

In manufacturing, many companies did not start quality programs until they had no other choice. Don't let yours be among the Information Age organizations that make the same mistake.

7.1   Take this personally

Data quality disasters need not be played out in public to damage a career. Providing misleading reports to management based on faulty data, is a sure-fire way to do so as well. So is failing to provide for data quality in a data warehouse project.

Field Tip 7.1: One goal of the data quality program should be to prevent embarrassment, both personal or organizational, both internally or publicly.

---

8.   E-Commerce Report, "On the Web, Pricing Errors Can Be Costly In More Ways Than One," *The New York Times*, December 13, 1999.
9.   Saul Hansell, "As Sales Boom Online, Some Customers Boo; Electronic Traffic is Up, But Customer Satisfaction is Heading South," *The New York Times*, December 17, 1999.

8

Poor Data Quality Can Be Insidious

Insidious, a. 1. Characterized by treachery or slyness; crafty; wily. 2. Operating in a slow or not easily apparent manner; more dangerous than seems evident.

Poor quality data and their impact make headlines from time to time. Many examples were cited in Chapter 7.

But let's face it. Most people don't think about data or data quality too often or too hard. Instead we go about our daily lives. We take orders and deliver goods and services to customers. We bill them and collect revenue. We improve existing goods and services and market and sell them. We manage the organization. We try to figure out e-business. We make decisions and we plan. We report on how we're doing and we try to do better. We seek satisfaction on the job and try to make the jobs of others more satisfying. We try to gain a competitive advantage.

And data underlie almost everything we do. Indeed, virtually every activity the Information Age organization undertakes requires data in some form or fashion. But still we don't think much about data.

There are many reasons for this. First, none of the activities noted above is really *about* data. Though each requires data, in some cases enormous amounts of data, and each creates new data, the primary results are not data. Instead, the hoped-for results are a satisfied customer, more revenue, a good decision, a better product, a better plan, a more satisfied employee, and so forth.

Second, the data are invisible. You don't really touch the data per se. You may access a database, read numbers on a spreadsheet, or receive a report full of numbers. All contain a representation of data, but they aren't as tangible or immediate as the task at hand.

Third, individuals may recognize that poor data hinder their work. The order taker may be frustrated that he or she has to correct so many customer addresses, which slows him or her down. The crew on the loading dock may curse management for not getting the loading instructions right; the marketer may wonder why so much direct mail comes back as "undeliverable." And the decision maker may wonder when the next set of numbers will come in so he or she can finish the recommendation report.

Each person is concerned about the data he or she uses. But few are concerned enough to worry about how the next guy will be impacted by the data he or she creates. Somehow, dealing with the bad data one is given is just part of the job. But bad data are like a virus. Unless confined, there is no telling where they will turn up.

Entire departments are created to deal with poor quality data, though they are seldom recognized as such. There is an entire industry whose sole function is to identify services that hospitals "forgot" to bill. Other examples include the portions of accounts payable that correct errant supplier invoices and customer service departments that spend their time correcting billing errors.

Customer billing provides a good illustration of an important data quality issue about which most organizations seem ignorant. As noted in Chapter 3, billing errors fall into two categories: overbilling, in which the customer is billed more that he or she should be, and underbilling, in which the customer is billed less. Customers are concerned about overbilling and demand a correction when they detect an error. Many companies keep track of the revenue they must give back to customers. It may be about one percent of revenue.

They have no similar window into underbilling. One of the two following situations must be true:

1.   The billing system is biased, systematically overbilling customers and letting them find the errors, if they can. Few companies would admit this to be the case.

2.   The billing system is not biased. Then the underbilling is about equal to the overbilling. And the company is forfeiting one percent of revenue. A pretty large impact for a single problem.

3.   Of course, it is convenient to blame the information technology department. After all, those data are just "part of the new system, which replaced the old system, which didn't work any better."

Since accommodating bad data is just part of the job, accounting systems don't track their costs very well. Few organizations have conducted systematic studies to quantify how good or bad their data are (most don't even know what data they have). Table 8.1 summarizes current quality levels and the impact poor data have on the typical organization. The numbers presented here are not scientifically defensible. They do not represent a cross-section of modern business or types of data, nor are they the product of a controlled study (if anything, these numbers may be more optimistic since they come from organizations that were at least concerned about the subject). But they do present a fair point of departure.

Few people challenge the facts presented in Table 8.1. Instead, people seem to sense, one way or another, that gross (meaning both large and ugly) problems stem directly from poor data quality. The last section of Table 8.1, describing impact on business strategy, is most provocative. It is also the

Table 8.1   *The Impacts (Often Hidden) of Poor Quality Data on the Organization*

	On Operations
On Customer Satisfaction	Lessened. Customers are often unforgiving of simple data errors.
On Cost	Increased. Upwards of 10% of revenue—for service organizations, up to 50% of expense is due to poor data quality.
On Employee Morale	Lowered. Dealing with errors is hard, unfulfilling work.
	On Decision-Making Tactics
Decision-making Capability	Reduced. Poorer, less-confident decisions that take longer to make
Data Warehouses	Delayed implementation
Reengineering	Poor quality is a major impediment.
Trust between Organizations	Dramatically lowered
On Labor Pool	Skilled employees required for non–value-added work.*
	On Strategy
Setting Strategy	Take longer and is more difficult
Execution	More difficult due to impact on operations and tactics
Ability to Derive Value from Data	Contributing factor to reduce ability. Exacerbates issues of data ownership.
Ability to Align the Organization	Compromised. Data don't align, so departments can't talk to one another.
Management Attention	Diverted from other issues

*Recent tightening of the labor market may make it difficult to find skilled workers willing to perform non–value-added work.

most difficult to observe directly. Yet it is evident that poor data quality will hinder strategy in dozens of insidious ways. Indeed, it is hard to imagine the following scenarios:

- An effective strategy of customer intimacy[1] if data that describe it are incorrect, out-of-date, "not quite relevant," or don't paint a comprehensive view of customers

- An effective strategy of cost leadership if the organization must bear the expense of correcting simple data errors

- An effective strategy of product leadership if the current product inventory is out-of-date

Don't expect data quality to be easy to spot. Instead, look for poor data quality as a contributing cause to the organization's most important business problems.

Field Tip 8.1: Most important data quality problems don't present themselves as such. Identify them through their impact on the organization's most important business objectives.

---

1.   These three strategies are those described by Michael Treacy and Fred Wiersma. Michael Treacy and Fred Wiersma, *The Discipline of Market Leaders* (Reading, MA: Addison-Wesley, 1995), p. 125.

9

Seek Competitive Advantage Through Quality Data

Obviously enough, improved data quality can eliminate most of the issues raised in Chapter 7 and ease those raised in Chapter 8. Experience confirms that one to two orders of magnitude improvement can be made. And while accounting systems are not geared to measure the costs of poor data quality, many successful projects report, somewhat informally, cost reductions of 66 percent to 75 percent. These estimates include total, easily measurable cost. Thus, if department A creates data to be used by department B, improved data can dramatically reduce the costs incurred by department B. Importantly, A's costs are often reduced as well, because it spends less time helping B resolve specific errors. In most cases, as we shall see, both departments have to invest a small amount of money in a "data quality system," to make sure that B's requirements are clear and understood, to identify and resolve the most important problems, and to measure progress. This investment is small compared with the total savings, yielding the 66 to 75 percent reductions cited previously.

These estimates do not include more subtle factors, such as the improved relationships between departments A and B. Data quality efforts focus the departments and help build trust between them. In time, their abilities to work together improve dramatically. This trust may be even more critical if departments A and B are different companies, and B is A's customer. Company A naturally wants excellent customer relationships, and company B naturally wants outstanding suppliers it can trust over the long haul.

It is extremely difficult to put a dollar estimate on "trust" and the "ability to work together" and we will not try to do so here. But the benefits are enormous and most people accept the fact that if a dollar estimate could be reliably determined, it would be far greater than the cost reduction.

Poor quality data also impacts decision making. While erred data can obviously contribute to a poor decision, experience suggests a more subtle effect. Rather, decision makers don't trust data. They move cautiously as a result. They seek confirmatory data, which adds time and confusion (to quote Mark Twain, "A man with a watch knows what time it is. A man with two is never sure."). And it is more difficult to align the organization to the decision.

Trusted data allow decision makers to move forward with confidence, speed, and power. We do not wish to suggest that the best possible data will eliminate all risk in decision making (indeed, since the results of decisions occur in the future, risk is inherent to decision making). But the best possible data eliminate one important factor. Further, execution is often more important than the decision itself. And an aligned organization executes better.

Finally, high quality data facilitate many Information Age strategies. The ability to deliver quickly is one. You simply can't move quickly if you have to check data in the middle of a process, project, or decision. The ability to build strong customer relationships is another. Unless the organization has only a few customers, its knowledge of the customer is bound up in its data. So relevant, comprehensive, correct, and up-to-date customer data are essential. Finally, the Internet and e-commerce not only make heretofore proprietary data available to customers, but require customers to use those data. On the one hand, poor data quality can destroy fledgling customer relationships. On the other, higher than expected data quality can lead to competitive advantage.

It is evident that improved data quality yields competitive advantage. The company with the best data can get closer to customers; keep costs down; make faster, more confident decisions; execute better; and respond more quickly and flexibly. It's not one silver bullet that yields the advantage, but the combination of many small factors. Indeed, it is evident that the company that takes full advantage of its Information Age assets, data, information, and knowledge has a bright future.

The history of the penetration of quality into manufacturing is instructive. It teaches that, sooner or later, customers demand quality of every industry. Companies have two choices: They can be the first in their industry to seek competitive advantage through data quality or they can wait until the consequences of not doing so are dire.

Not all of these benefits are of equal importance to every organization. In building the business case, it is expedient to focus on the two or three things that the organization cares about most. Start by articulating the organization's most important business problems, opportunities, and directions.

Then cite how improved data can mitigate those problems, advance the opportunities, and enhance the selected directions.

Field Tip 9.1: In developing the case for data quality, demonstrate how improvements will lead to competitive advantage.

The Heart of the Matter

There seem to be hundreds of ways to improve data quality, but most are simply variants of the following two major approaches:

1. Finding and fixing errors (clean-up)

2. Preventing errors

This section describes these two approaches (Chapter 10), and the likely results of diligent execution of each (Chapter 11); examines the role the rate of new data collection plays in making the best choice (Chapter 12); and develops four simple rules that summarize approaches that lead to the best results, given the organization's particular circumstances (Chapter 13).

A Database Is Like a Lake

A useful analogy that illustrates the possible approaches to many data quality problems/opportunities is illustrated in Figure 10.1. In the analogy, a lake represents a database. The database need not be a massive electronic database, the analogy works just as well with a simple one-page spreadsheet. Further in the analogy, the lake water represents the data, the stream or streams feeding the lake represent information chains that create the data, and the factories upstream represent sources of pollutant. Not pictured, but important to the analogy, is a person drinking the lake water. This person represents a "data customer," someone using the data to complete some operation, make a decision, or plan.

Figure 10.1   *To clean up the lake, one must first eliminate the sources of pollution*

Faced with a polluted lake, one has four choices:

1. Ignore the pollutants and treat those who get sick from the lake water.

2. Filter the lake water, remove the sources of pollutant, and put the water back in the lake.

3. Filter small amounts of water each day. One could filter water at the point of entry into the lake. Thus, only clean water enters the lake. Or one could filter water right before it is used.

4. Identify the sources of pollutant and eliminate (or at least mitigate) them.

Likewise, faced with a polluted database—one with numerous data errors—one has four choices:

1. Deal with the impacts of the erred data. These may involve correcting bad decisions, soothing angry customers (and giving them their money back), and letting organizational mistrust simmer.

2. Conduct database clean-ups, in one of their various guises. These guises involve surveying customers, comparing one database with another and investigating discrepancies, and running automated tests to identify data that don't conform to "business rules."

3. Conduct small database clean-ups daily as part of everyday operations. Thus, one could clean up data upon entry into a database. Or one could clean up data prior to using them.

4. Determine the sources of erred data upstream, in the information chains that create the new data.

The first, and most important, choice that an organization must make is which of these general approaches to take. An organization that has patently ignored data quality has implicitly selected the first option. Given evidence that data are erred, organizations do not knowingly select this approach. (Of course, no matter how clean the data, an occasional error may slip through. And the impact must be treated!)

As a practical matter, the choice involves the latter three options. Each has its plusses and minuses. To briefly summarize, option 2 is the most frequently selected. There are any number of good computer tools that can automate error detection and many Information Technology departments are skilled at using them. Error correction is more problematic, but it can often be farmed out to relatively low-paid temps. Further, everyone seems to have an intuitive sense of what clean-up is and can rally around the clean-up project. Finally, while data clean-up is certainly not easy, the job can be fairly well delineated and completed in a reasonable amount of time. People and organizations seem to derive a sense of satisfaction from database clean-up.

The principal drawback is that database clean-up alone almost never works over the long haul. The reason is quite simple—just as those streams keep putting new, polluted water into the lake, so too do information chains introduce erred data into the database. New data are created with stunning rapidity in many cases. Customer billing, often on a monthly cycle, is a good example. By the end of the month a whole new collection of erred invoices has been created. And data clean-up never ends.

Other drawbacks of this approach are its enormous expense and the false sense of security it gives that these data are correct. The reason for this is that error detection tools only identify obvious errors. Thus, they can identify that a record containing AREA CODE = 212 (New York City) and ZIP CODE = 90210 (Hollywood, CA) has at least one error. But many errors don't violate any simple rule and so escape detection. Unfortunately, cleaned data are advertised just that way, and data customers assume all values are correct.

The third option—cleaning up a small portion of data each day—is sometimes called "data editing." As with lake water, there are two basic styles: cleaning up the new data created daily and cleaning up the data before they are used. In effect, clean-up simply becomes part of ongoing operations. Organizations that depend on the most current data (e.g., the price of a security to a brokerage house) often elect this approach.

The fourth option involves identifying and detecting the root causes of errors and eliminating them. Note that the *focus shifts from detecting and correcting errors that have already occurred to preventing future errors*. This approach has obvious long-term advantages. Done with care, many organizations can reduce their rates of error creation by factors of 10–100 (i.e., if the previous error rate was 5 percent, it can be reduced to .5–.05 percent—in other words, data that were 95 percent accurate, become 99.9–99.95 percent accurate). Further, experience teaches that most errors stem from relatively simple causes—ill-informed or poorly trained staff, lack of clear instructions, and the like—which can be eliminated relatively easily.

The principal drawback is that people and organizations, in the rush to get through the day, tend not to think much about root causes. And, indeed, the root cause of an error that impacts the billing department may occur far upstream in order entry. It can be hard to reach out to other organizations not under one's control.

Field Tip 10.1: Don't be misled. Finding and correcting errors is non–value-added work. It is difficult, expensive, and time-consuming as well. Most importantly, it doesn't work very well.

Likely Outcomes

There is very little mystery in data quality. Each of the approaches described in Chapter 10 leads to predictable improvements in data quality and predictable benefits to the organization (since the benefits are a function of the improvements). These are summarized in the plots shown in Figures 11.1, 11.2, and 11.3 (one each for options 2–4). Each plot features the predicted quality level of both the database (i.e., the lake) and the information chain feeding it (i.e., the stream) in time.

The two most pertinent conclusions from these figures are as follows:

1.   Over time, options 2 and 3 (forms of clean-ups) do not address the upstream information chains, so they never improve.

2.   Option 4 (preventing errors) does not address existing data. But, over time, new, high-quality data replace old, erred data, and the quality of the database improves. Importantly (though not illustrated in the figures) experience confirms that in most cases newer data are more useful to the organization than old data.

The figures illustrate two other points. One of the criticisms leveled against option 4 is that it takes too long to get started. Since computer routines to detect errors can be run overnight, it seems evident that the clean-up options take less time. But start-up must also be considered. Start-up time for clean-up involves buying or building the needed computer tools and training people to use them. Even more importantly, start-up also involves deciding how errors will be corrected (another insidious data quality problem). Figuring out how to correct errors is a messier problem than one might think. So start-up time is often much longer than expected.

Start-up time for the prevention approach is highly variable. It doesn't usually take very long (or cost very much) to train people and get them started. These people can usually identify a simple root cause of error fairly

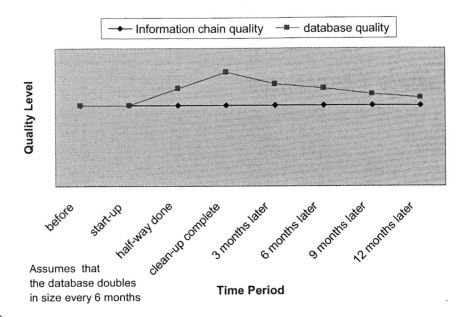

Figure 11.1   *Quality levels: Database clean-up (option 2)*

quickly. But, as previously noted, an organization may go through an enormous amount of time-consuming internal machinations before deciding to do so.

This point leads to a second important consideration, difficulty in getting started. Simply stated, many organizations are uncomfortable with the fourth option, preventing errors. It forces them to think and act differently.

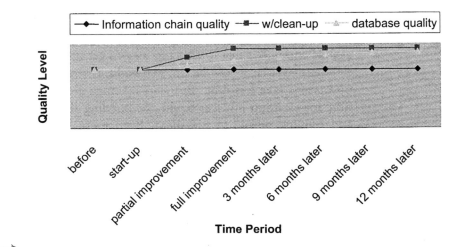

Figure 11.2   *Quality levels: Ongoing operations (option 3)*

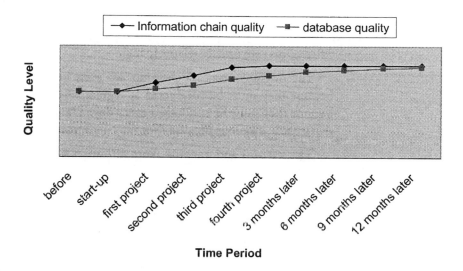

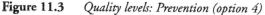

Figure 11.3   *Quality levels: Prevention (option 4)*

So aligning the organization to take this approach can prove difficult. Option 2, the database clean-up, is usually the easiest to start. Frequently a crisis precipitates interest in data quality and very senior managers take an active interest in solving it. Thus, "We can't get assembled product because the system says raw materials are there and they're not" can be a strong motivator to clean up the system.

A third factor is the cost of the data quality effort. As discussed in Chapter 8, when data quality efforts work, they yield fantastic payback. So cost is not usually of primary concern. Figure 11.4 plots start-up and ongoing costs associated with the data quality effort. In summary, the start-up costs

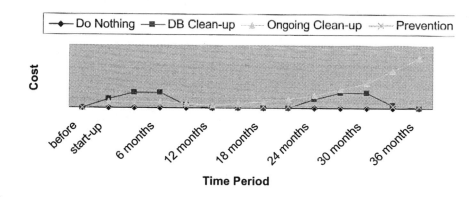

Figure 11.4   *Incremental cost of data quality efforts*

for both clean-up approaches are high. Tool costs (to buy or build the error detection tool) and people costs (to select the tool, use it, and correct identified errors) are usually relatively high.

The ongoing costs of clean-up are even higher—database clean-ups, because they must be conducted at regular intervals, and daily clean-ups, because they must be conducted every day. The costs of daily clean-ups are particularly insidious because they may get lost in the accounting system.

The start-up and ongoing costs of option 4, prevention, are comparatively low. The primary costs involve training people, allowing time for them to identify and eliminate issues, and so forth.

Field Tip 11.1: Don't be seduced by the glamour of fancy tools to clean up erred data. They may help in the short term, but over the long haul there is no substitute for preventing errors.

The Organic Nature of Data

Two other important factors bear on the choice of approach to data quality improvement. These are the rate of new data creation and the utility of the data. A third factor, data's expected lifetime, is a bit more subtle and sometimes also plays a role.

It is easy to think of data as the "stuff stored away in databases." For data quality at least, it is more useful to think of data as almost organic, coming into existence, getting stored and processed, used and modified, transmitted to other databases and further used and modified, and so on. Eventually, of course, all data outlive their usefulness. When they do, they have reached the ends of their useful lifetimes.

There are two kinds of information chains that create new data—those that define new types of data (i.e., new data models) and those that create new data values (either new entities or new values for existing entities). Both create new data at stunning rates in the Information Age. It is important that organizations get a handle on their rates of new data creation. Consider new data records. One good way to measure the rate of new data creation is "new records per day." Some examples are as follows:

- A patient in a hospital, through records of procedures performed, tests run, and drugs administered, may create dozens of new records each day. In total, a mid-size hospital may create thousands of new records each day.

- A financial services firm conducts 100,000 trades per day. Then the rate of new data creation for the Trades Database is 100,000 trades/day.

- If a person makes about five phone calls/day, then a minimum of five data records are created. Further, if a phone company has five million customers, making an average of five calls per day, then the database of phone calls grows at a rate of 25 million records per day.

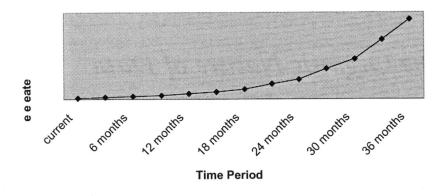

Figure 12.1   *Rates of new data creation*

Now suppose that even a small fraction of records, say 5 percent, contain an error. And few organizations are willing to claim that only 5 percent of their data records are erred, unless they have initiated a data quality program. Then the phone company creates 1.25 million erred records a day. If it elects one of the clean-up approaches, then it must identify and correct 1.25 million errors a day, just to stay even. A daunting challenge indeed.

A useful time-series plot features the rate of new data creation for the past several years and projections for the next few years. The plot usually looks like that shown in Figure 12.1. Clearly, in the not too distant future, the rate of new data creation will double, quadruple, and so on. Figure 12.1 reinforces the hollowness of data clean-up approaches. Even if one can keep up with today's errors, sooner or later their numbers overwhelm. Thus, in the language of computer scientists, clean-up approaches do not scale.

Now consider data's utility. It is evident that not all data are created equal—some are simply much more important. It is equally evident that data quality efforts should be directed at the most useful data. An organization's most critical business strategies usually point quite clearly to these data.

Somewhat more subtly, the subject of the least important data is also pertinent. Unfortunately, organizations create or otherwise acquire enormous quantities of data that are never used for anything. Some organizations estimate the fraction of data and/or management reports that are never used to be as high as 50 percent. From a quality standpoint, such data should simply be ignored. This is the first option discussed in Chapter 10. Better still, the organization should stop collecting them and use the savings to invest in the larger data quality effort.

Just as it is evident that database clean-up does nothing to address newly created data, prevention does nothing to correct already erred data. And, in some cases, already-erred data will remain important for a very long time. The best example is the BIRTHDATE field. The field is used for any number of purposes. And in most cases, there is no "upstream process" to erase and correct it if it is erred.

Thus, in some cases, a datum's "expected useful lifetime" is important. (Note that this datum's lifetime ends when it is no longer useful, not when it is actually destroyed. For data are seldom destroyed. In most situations, they hang around, cluttering up databases, and making it more difficult to find needed data.) Important data with long expected lifetimes must be cleaned up.

Field Tip 12.1: All data quality programs should focus first on the most important data.

Field Tip 12.2: The rate of new data creation is the most important factor in determining the best approach to data quality.

Field Tip 12.3: If funds are tight, make the data quality effort self-funding. A useful first step is to quit creating and/or acquiring data that are never used.

A note of caution

The subject of managing data throughout their lifetimes is interesting, subtle, and beyond the scope of this *Field Guide*. For example, there is great potential for data mining techniques to extend the useful lifetime of much data. Thus, this *Field Guide* does not advocate the planned destruction of data, especially data that have proven useful. Continuing to collect data that are not proving useful is another matter. When defining a new data structure, many organizations have a tendency to put everything in because it might be useful some day. While a few of those things may prove useful, most do not. But the organization continues to collect them. Even a casual look often reveals enormous amounts of data that have not been used, are not being used, that no one plans to use, and that no one even understands. Organizations should stop collecting these data. Aggressively!

13

Crafting the Approach

Previous chapters have reviewed factors involved in selecting the best approach for addressing data quality issues. To summarize, the following rules are all but obvious:

- Rule 1: Data that are not important should be ignored. The most important data, those critical to the organization's most important strategies, should be addressed first.

- Rule 2 (prevent, then clean): It is almost always best to adopt the prevention approach first (option 4). When upstream information chains or suppliers produce new data of acceptable quality, then data clean-ups, if they are still needed, can be focused on pockets of important data with long lifetimes.

- Rule 3: Data clean-up cannot produce satisfactory results over the long term. So data clean-up, in any of its guises, must never be used alone (with one exception, which is explained below).

The logic of rule 1 is simple. As long as one is going to the trouble to improve something, it might as well be something that matters. The logic of rule 3 is straightforward as well. Even if existing data have long lifetimes, such as BIRTHDATE, new data will still be created, and the only way to ensure they are of high quality is to prevent future errors. The only known exception involves a one-time scientific experiment, which will never be repeated (and hopefully these are rare). In that case it may be appropriate to clean up the data, the exceptional difficulties in determining correct values aside.

Rule 2 discusses the best approach to combining prevention and clean-up. By focusing first on prevention, the long-term problem is addressed. This also has the salutary effect of making the short-term problem of correcting already erred data smaller. Combining the two approaches in this way yields outstanding results.

There are a few important exceptions to the prevent-then-clean rule, but not as many as people think. All important exceptions involve serious damage to the organization and/or its employees. For example, if the organization cannot collect revenue because customers won't pay invoices they don't trust, then these invoices must be cleaned up. Or, if payroll is incorrect, this problem must also be cleaned up.

But even then, clean-up must not proceed alone—otherwise the problem will never go away. Even in such dire circumstances, organizations do well to follow the "dime for a dollar" guideline. It states that for every dollar spent cleaning up poor data, at least a dime should be spent preventing future errors.

Since the prevention approach does not produce the short-term excitement of clean-ups, many managers don't like it. Instead they try to seduce with statements such as "We'll clean the data first, then work the prevention process." While in principle this can work, it almost never does. Instead, having completed the clean-up, the manager is off to the next exciting topic and prevention never occurs. Instead, six to 24 months down the road, the database is once again severely erred and another clean-up is recommended. This leads to the fourth rule:

- Rule 4: If a data clean-up is required, take steps to ensure that it need never be repeated.

Rules 1–4 are summarized in Figure 13.1.

We wish to emphasize how rare exceptions to the prevent then clean rule really are. Developers of databases, particularly data warehouses, often argue that migrating data to a data warehouse is one. But this is simply not so. A well-planned migration should focus on data quality months in advance of

Rule 1: Focus on those data most critical to the organization's most important strategies first. Ignore data that are not used.

Rule 2 (prevent, then clean): Prevent future errors by improving upstream information chains and suppliers first. When these data sources are of acceptable quality, target clean-ups at important pockets of long-lasting data.

Rule 3: Data clean-up by itself is almost never a viable long-term strategy.

Rule 4: If clean-up is required, make sure it is NEVER repeated.

Figure 13.1   *Summary of rules for selecting the appropriate approach to data quality*

the physical migration. It will be necessary to transform or reformat data, but not to correct many errors.

Similarly, many organizations recognize shortcomings in their data resource data—that is, their data that describe other data. Data resource data explains, for example, that an ADJUSTED CURRENCY field is expressed in 1995 United States dollars. Developers (and others) are sometimes too casual about ensuring they produce high-quality data resource data. The result is that data are subject to misinterpretation. Indeed, some organizations lack data resource data altogether and resolve to right this wrong through a clean-up. But it violates the rules.

Field Tip 13.1: First, *prevent future errors, then clean up existing errors.* Unless circumstances are dire, resist efforts to compromise on this point.

D

Necessary Background

This section provides background needed to better understand the rest of this Field Guide. More importantly, this background provides necessary foundations on which to build the organization's data quality program. The first chapter (Chapter 14) defines data, data quality, other important terms. Dry as definitions can be, most people have entrenched, though not well thought out, ideas about these concepts. Getting people to think more broadly about and adopting common definitions of key terms is no small feat.

A second chapter (Chapter 15) develops the concept of a "second-generation data quality system." Those organizations with the best quality data make use of these systems. They employ a number of common elements, each crafted to suit their particular circumstances. These common elements are the subjects of Sections E, F, and G.

The third chapter (Chapter 16) describes the so-called "customer-supplier model," perhaps the most important organizing framework for all of quality management.

14

Data and Data Quality Defined

The concept of "data" can be tricky. Indeed, many competing definitions (such as "data are the raw materials for information") miss the structure inherent in data. For the purpose of this *Field Guide*, "data" (or a "collection of data," etc.) consist of two interrelated components, "data models" and "data values." "Data models" define what the data are all about. Generally data describe an "entity," some real-world object or abstraction, such as a CUSTOMER, EMPLOYEE, or SALE. Attributes and relationships describe pertinent features of the entities. NAME, BIRTHDATE, and ITEM DESCRIPTION, respectively, may be features of interest. "Data values" are assigned to attributes in the data model for specified entities. The "September 7, 1954" in EMPLOYEE BIRTHDATE = September 7, 1954, is a data value for a specified employee.

The reason a data model is so named is because it models some aspect of the real world using data. Different organizations usually are interested in different features of the world, so they use different data models. For example, an employer may be interested in the reader as an EMPLOYEE, the IRS as a TAXPAYER. The reader is the same real-world entity in both cases, but the employer and the IRS are interested in different things about the reader. Both need NAME and SOCIAL SECURITY NUMBER. The IRS needs INTEREST INCOME, DIVIDENDS, and other attributes pertinent to tax collection. The employer needs COLLEGE, DEGREE, and other attributes pertinent to the job.

Note that data, as defined previously, are intangible. You can't touch data in the usual sense.

Nor must data values be correct. Indeed, simple observation confirms they are frequently wrong. So it is improper to call data "facts" unless one is certain they are correct.

Four distinct activities (at least) impact the quality of even the simplest data: modeling, creation of data values, storage/access, and formatting of whatever is presented.

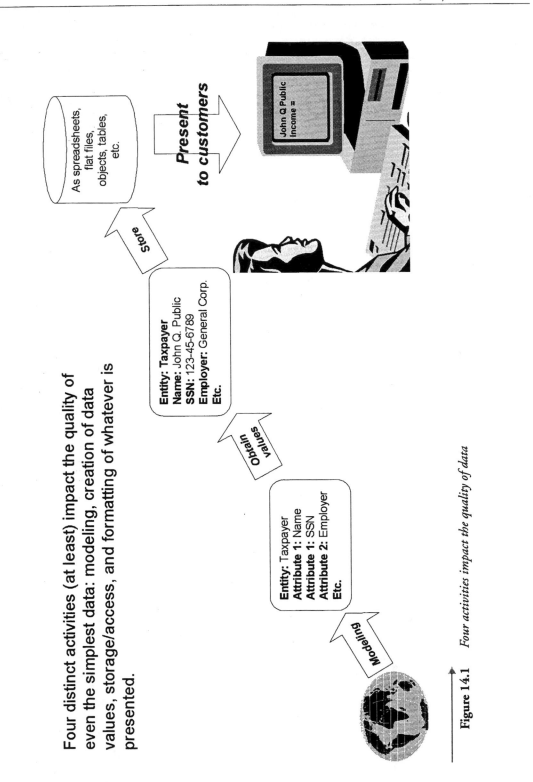

As spreadsheets, flat files, objects, tables, etc.

Present to customers

John Q Public Income =

Store

Entity: Taxpayer
Name: John Q. Public
SSN: 123-45-6789
Employer: General Corp.
Etc.

Obtain values

Entity: Taxpayer
Attribute 1: Name
Attribute 1: SSN
Attribute 2: Employer
Etc.

Modeling

Figure 14.1   *Four activities impact the quality of data*

"Data records," as distinct from data per se, are the physical realizations of these data stored in paper files, in spreadsheets, or in databases. Data records may be presented to users in different ways that do not change the underlying data. We call data records that are presented (as opposed to simply stored) to data customers "data products" or sometimes "information products." Note that data (i.e., the models and values) are abstract, while data records and information products are their tangible realizations. Data resource data or metadata are those data that describe other data. These definitions are summarized in Figure 14.1.

Now consider the term "quality." In the early 1980s, an interesting debate involved whether a VW Bug or a Cadillac was of higher quality. Some favored the Bug for its reliability; others the Cadillac for its creature comforts. The following four main points evolved from the debate:

1. The VW appeared to have fewer "bugs" (no pun intended) compared with the Cadillac.

2. The Cadillac was certainly more luxurious, handled better, and had more room for luggage.

3. Different people had different needs. The Cadillac better met the needs of some people, the VW of others.

4. Quality involved perceptions. The VW may or may not have really had fewer defects. But that was certainly the perception. And relatively few people bothered to check published statistics.

These points lead to the following definition of data quality (based on Joseph Juran):

Data are of high quality if they are fit for their intended uses in operations, decision making, and planning. Data are fit for use if they are free of defects and possess desired features. (See Figure 14.2)

Note first, that data quality is intimately tied to customers and their uses of data. In a very real sense "data are of high quality if those who use them say so." Chapter 17 provides a step-by-step process for understanding customer needs.

Second, data may be put to any number of uses. And it almost always happens that data that are ideally fit for one use are marginally fit for a second and poorly fit for a third. The IRS would not find EMPLOYEE data sufficient to do its job. So, to the IRS these data are of poor quality, even though they suit the employer perfectly. Data quality is not a concept that makes sense "in the average." It is about meeting the specific needs of specific customers.

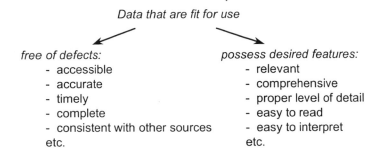

Data are of high quality if they are fit for their intended
uses in operations, decision making, and planning
(after Joseph Juran).

Data that are fit for use

free of defects: possess desired features:
  - accessible   - relevant
  - accurate   - comprehensive
  - timely   - proper level of detail
  - complete   - easy to read
  - consistent with other sources   - easy to interpret
  etc.   etc.

Figure 14.2   *Data quality defined*

Third, customers see defects as including inaccurate data, data that are
out-of-date, data that are hard to interpret, and so forth. Customers most
often see "erred data values" as defective. Generally a data supplier does not
get much credit for providing defect-free data. But defective data produce
enormous customer dissatisfaction.

But defect-free data are generally not enough. Data must possess features
that make it easier for the data customer to conduct an operation, make a
decision, or plan. Data that are relevant, comprehensive, give the proper
level of detail, and so on, possess desired features. In most cases, the features
are determined by the data model. For example, the relevancy of data is a
direct result of the data model. By providing needed features, data providers
can create customer satisfaction.

Field Tip 14.1: Data are only of high quality if those who use them say so.
Usually high-quality data must be both free of defects and possess features
that customers desire.

15

Second-Generation Data Quality Systems

By the phrase "data quality system (DQS)," we mean the totality of an organization's efforts that bear on data quality. Note specifically that the term "system" does not refer to computer or database systems, though of course computers and databases are often elements of the overall data quality system.

The totality of effort is large in most organizations. It includes the work and supporting management associated with the following:

- Correcting errors and other deficiencies that customers and others outside the organization find. Remedy the impact by shipping new product, refunding payment, paying contractual penalties, and so forth — essentially all the things associated with option 1 of Chapter 10.

- Conducting periodic database clean-ups (option 2 of Chapter 10).

- Conducting daily clean-ups as part of operations (option 3).

- Preventing errors (option 4).

As a simple observation, the DQSs of most organizations include the first three components. Such DQSs are often called *first-generation data quality systems* because they employ the paradigm of finding and correcting errors, or data clean-up. DQSs that (largely) employ the paradigm of preventing errors (option 4) are called *second-generation data quality systems* (see Figure 15.1). For a DQS to qualify as second-generation, we do not require that there be no clean-up activities. We do require, however, that the "prevention mentality" predominate. (Indeed, it is ludicrous to think that an organization would not correct an error brought to its attention by a customer, no matter how vigilant its efforts to prevent such errors. It must correct such errors cheerfully, and it must make good on promises that were not kept due to bad data.)

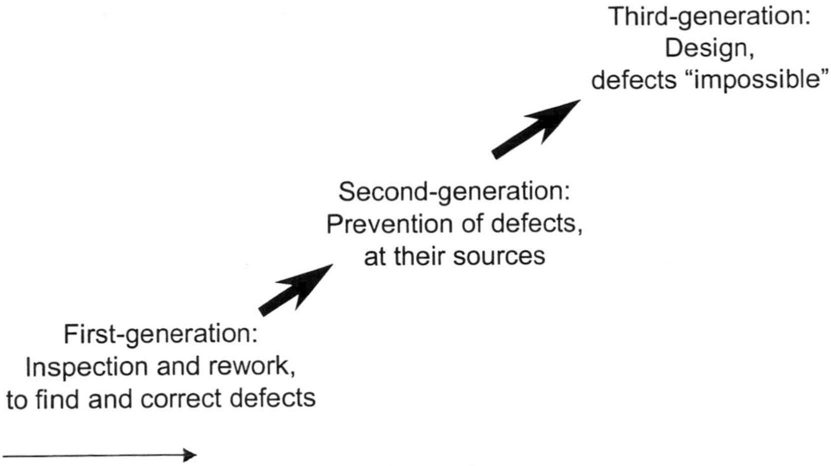

Third-generation:
Design,
defects "impossible"

Second-generation:
Prevention of defects,
at their sources

First-generation:
Inspection and rework,
to find and correct defects

Figure 15.1   *Approaches to data quality*

"Paradigms" are models or patterns of thought, often embedded deep in an individual's or organization's mind. They represent reflexive ways of thinking. Importantly, once an idea has reached paradigm status, it is very difficult to change. In a particularly acid comment, Max Planck once remarked that "a new scientific truth does not triumph by convincing its opponents and making them see the light, but rather because its opponents eventually die, and a new generation goes up that is familiar with it." [1]

In many organizations, due to the strength of the clean-up paradigm, the immediate response to a data quality problem is to "get better or faster at cleaning up data." Unfortunately, as shown in Chapters 11–13, there is usually not enough clean-up horsepower to get the job done. The hard part of preventing errors is not technical. Rather, it is to overcome the emotional and intellectual investment in data clean-up. Practical advice for doing so is presented in Chapters 33 and 34.

Figure 15.1 also shows third-generation DQSs based on a philosophy of making it impossible, or at least very difficult, to make errors. We know of no organization that employs a third-generation DQS at this time, but we look forward to them. In manufacturing and other areas where the quality systems are more advanced than for data, third-generation quality systems have led to so-called "six-sigma" quality levels (3.4 defects per million).

Another useful concept is that of an "information chain." Figure 15.2 presents a generic information chain. Essentially an information chain is an end-to-end process that starts with original data sources, creates "informa-

1.   Max Planck, *Scientific Autobiography and Other Papers*, trans. F. Gaynor (New York, 1949), pp. 33–34.

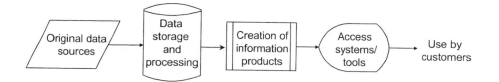

High data quality requires:
- Clear understanding of customers and their needs
- Horizontal management of information chains
- Responsibility for data quality at original sources
- End-to-end measurement
- Continual improvement

Figure 15.2   *Generic information chain*

tion products" and continues through to the use of data in operations, decision-making, and planning. It includes supporting technologies such as databases and access tools. A simple information chain for a mail-order company might involve the creation, processing, and use of data to:

- Take a customer's order

- Collect the ordered items from the warehouse and package them for delivery

- Invoice the customer, collect payment, and credit the customer's account

A second information chain might involve creation, processing, and use of the data to:

- Determine which "styles" are most popular

- Plan the next catalog to emphasize those styles

- Forecast needed quantities of each item and arrange for supply

Information chains are long, skinny, flows of data and information that wind their way, department by department, across an organization. We shall see that managing them is essential to effective second-generation DQSs.

A final important concept is that of "value-added" versus "non-value-added work." For all practical purposes, work is value-added if customers are willing to pay for it and non-value-added otherwise. Thus most customers are willing to pay for data products, but they are not willing to pay extra for someone to find and correct underlying data errors.

Management Infrastructure

- Data Quality Council*
- Data Quality Vision
- Data Quality Policy*
- Business Case for Data Quality
- Data Supplier Management*
- Information Chain Management*
- Innovation
- Standardization
- Management of Data Culture*
- Database of Record
- Strategic Data Quality Management
- Training and Education

Technical Capabilities

- ID of Information Chains
- Information Chain Description
- Customer Needs Analysis*
- Measurement*
- Quality Control*
- Quality Planning*
- Quality Improvement*
- Information (Re)Design
- Inspection and Test (Data Editing)
- Quality Assurance
- Document Assurance
- Rewards and Recognition
- Domain Knowledge
- Standards
- Quality Handbook

* Elements common to most successful data quality programs

Figure 15.3   *Second-generation data quality systems are crafted from common elements*

This concept embraces some important subtleties. Customers may well be willing, even desirous, of paying more for higher-quality data. Doing so saves them the added time and expense of finding the errors themselves. In total, higher quality data costs them less.

Most of this book is about second-generation DQSs—there are lots of good ones out there—and breaks them down into their constituent elements (see Figure 15.3). Figures 15.4–15.30 give short descriptions of each element. Each organization must pick and choose the elements best suited to its specific circumstance and meld them into a coherent system.

That said, ten elements are common to most successful programs. They reinforce each other to form a coherent "system," as illustrated in Figure 15.31. These are the subjects of Sections E, F, and G.

Field Tip 15.1: Do not underestimate how strongly individuals and organizations will cling to their beliefs in data clean-up. Don't be misled—clean-up is non-value-added work.

Definition: The senior management body charged with executing the data quality policy at the highest level. Responsible for setting quality goals, selecting "projects," providing training, and so forth. Responsible for estimating costs and benefits of quality function. May also feature a hierarchy of functional councils.

Motivation/Advantages:

- Emphasizes senior management commitment to quality.
- Provides the cross-functional coordination and support necessary to carry out the policy and projects.

Second-Generation Characteristics:

- Very senior, with broad representation.

Figure 15.4   *Data quality council (common to most successful data quality programs)*

Definition: A "picture" of the organization's desired future state with respect to data and information, including a rationale for people to work to create that future state. The data quality vision supports and enhances the organization's overall vision.

Motivation/Advantages:

- Forces organization to think about its long-term data and information needs and their connection to business success.
- Broad communication and alignment.
- Motivates action in the right direction.
- Provides basis for decision making.

Second-Generation Characteristics:

- Close coupling of desired future states of the business and data/information.
- Described in terms of benefits to the organization and its customers.

Figure 15.5   *Data quality vision*

Definition: A statement of management's intent regarding data and information quality, the organization's long-term data and information quality improvement objectives, and specific management accountabilities for pursuing the intent and achieving the objectives. The policy is intended as a "guide for managerial action."

Motivation/Advantages:
- Forces organization to think broadly and deeply about quality.
- Provides insiders and outsiders a superior form of "predictability."
- Broad communication and alignment.
- Reduces "lone ranger" mentality.

Second-Generation Characteristics:
- Recognizes data and information "as business assets."
- Delineates accountabilities along information chains.

Figure 15.6 *Data quality policy (common to most successful data quality programs)*

Definition: A summary of the business rationale for improving data quality, short- and mid-term objectives, and approach(es) selected.

Motivation/Advantages:
- Forces the enterprise to be clear about its objectives:
    - cost reduction
    - customer service
    - improved decision making
- Demonstrates need through cost/benefit analysis.
- Helps align decision makers

Second-Generation Characteristics:
- Clearly outlines and motivates second-generation data quality systems.
- Delineates early opportunities.
- Provides some seed money, but expects data quality program to be self-funding.

Figure 15.7 *Business case for data quality*

Definition: The overall program for managing suppliers, including selecting suppliers, ensuring that these suppliers understand what is expected, measuring performance against these expectations, and making improvements to close gaps.

Motivation/Advantages:

- Much data comes from suppliers. It is too difficult to find and correct errors downstream.
- Predictable input into information chains.

Second-Generation Characteristics:

- "Partnerships" built with the most important suppliers.
- Expectations documented.
- Data quality measurements made by suppliers and regularly communicated to customers.
- Focus on "rate of improvement" rather than actual level.

Figure 15.8 *Data supplier management (common to most successful data quality programs)*

Definition: Management infrastructure and technique intended to ensure accountability for the performance of cross-functional information chains.

Motivation/Advantages:

- Data and information cross organizational boundaries as information products are created.
- Most "problems" and/or opportunities occur on boundaries.
- Proven methods for making and sustaining improvements.
- "Control" yields predictable performance.

Second-Generation Characteristics:

- Information chains broadly defined.
- "Owners" have wide latitude for action, control, improvement.
- Customers and their needs documented and communicated.
- Overall measurement of most important quality dimensions.
- Continuous improvement.

Figure 15.9 *Information chain management (common to most successful data quality programs)*

Definition: Management infrastructure and technique to systematically define new data and information products and create business advantage.

Motivation/Advantages:

- New data, or exactly the right data, a source of competitive advantage.
- New ways of looking at data (data mining) yield new value from "old" data.
- "Informationalize" product and service.
- See also quality planning and improvement.

Second-Generation Characteristics:

- Innovation managed end-to-end, like any other information chain.
- Close connection to customer.

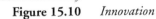

Figure 15.10   *Innovation*

Definition: Management infrastructure and technique to systematically define and implement common data definitions, procedures, etc.

Motivation/Advantages:

- Common definitions of key terms (such as "revenue") promote communication and alignment.
- Other common definitions (such as "customer") can create new opportunities.
- Other standards (e.g., measuring an "error rate") promote cross-organizational comparison.

Second-Generation Characteristics:

- Standards managed as an information chain, from nomination through development, through implementation.
- Used selectively. Recognition that standards are source of contention.

Figure 15.11   *Standardization*

Definition: Management infrastructure and technique intended to ensure that the enterprise is ready for and can adopt and make use of second-generation techniques, which promote management of data and information as business assets and which obviate or mitigate power struggles.

Motivation/Advantages:

- Most enterprises/organizations have first-generation data quality systems. Second-generation systems require them to think and act differently.
- Experience shows that change is always risky, but risks can be managed and/or reduced.
- Data engender politics and passions like no other resource.

Second-Generation Characteristics:

- The responsibility of the data council.
- Change actively managed and based on an accepted change model.
- Leaders actively supported. People given adequate support as their jobs change.
- Unwinnable battles avoided.

Figure 15.12 *Management of the data culture (common to most successful data quality programs)*

Definition: A data quality program through which the manager (or custodian) of a database (or portion thereof) satisfies agreed-upon quality criteria (e.g., accuracy > 99.5%) and is designated as the "approved master source" for that data.

Motivation/Advantages:

- Enterprise can assure itself that certain data are of high quality.
- Helps manage and reduce redundancy.
- Especially useful for common data such as customer data, employee data, etc.
- In many cases, any number of information chains traverse a given database. Stewardship provides a means to coordinate their needs. Information chain owners may be customers of and/or suppliers to the data steward.
- Stewards have clear standards to work toward.

Second-Generation Characteristics:

- Second-generation standards (i.e., focus is on measurement, error prevention, etc.).

Figure 15.13 *Databases of record (DBOR)*

Definition: A program that aims to ensure that the enterprise's top-line business strategy is "data enabled," that the enterprise has the data and information assets (especially data sources, information chains, and the ability to exploit them) to effect its strategy.

Motivation/Advantages:

- Data and information assets are the critical assets of the Information Age. Those who manage them have a distinct advantage.
- Data and information are related to strategy and not bound up with information technology.

Second-Generation Characteristics:

- This linkage is not evident in first-generation systems.

Figure 15.14   *Strategic data quality managment*

Definition: The program for ensuring that all involved have the knowledge, skills, and tools needed to do their jobs.

Motivation/Advantages:

- People must have the background and tools to carry out their assignments.
- Alignment.

Second-Generation Characteristics:

- Training is broad and deep.
- Much is conducted "on the job."
- Continuous; and budgeted at ~5% of payroll/work week.

Figure 15.15   *Training and education*

Definition: A process (either formal or informal) of identifying the data assets (i.e., data and information chains) most critical to the enterprise.

Motivation/Advantages:

- Not all data assets are created equal. Focuses attention on the most-important assets.

Second-Generation Characteristics:

- Business ⟶ Data ⟶ Information Chains ⟶ Original Sources

Figure 15.16 *Identification of information chains*

Definition: A description, usually formal, of an information chain's suppliers, the steps taken to produce information products, customers, and all other aspects (including data, organization, supporting technologies, etc.) that may impact performance.

Motivation/Advantages:

- The simple act of describing what is actually happening often surfaces incongruities.
- Improvement consists of changes to the information chain, to better meet needs of specific customers.
- Key steps can be measured and controlled.

Second-Generation Characteristics:

- The responsibility of the information chain owner.

Figure 15.17 *Information chain description*

Definition: A process (hopefully formal) of:
- Identifying and documenting customers and their needs.
- Communicating to those who need to know.
- Prioritizing those needs.

Motivation/Advantages:
- The customer is the final arbiter of quality.
- Alignment of those working on information chains in the direction of customer needs.
- Identifies needed planning and improvement projects.

Second-Generation Characteristics:
- Customer needs are formally documented and under change control.
- This task is the responsibility of information chain owners.

Figure 15.18   *Customer needs analysis (common to most successful data quality programs)*

Definitions:

At the information chain level: The *process* of quantifying information chain performance, including alignment of measures to customer needs, development of a measurement protocol, data collection, and interpretation of results.

At the enterprise level: An overall system or collection of measurement processes.

Other common definitions not used here: The *act* of data collection or the *resultant number.*

Motivation/Advantages:
- Replaces opinion with fact.
- Quantification of costs, benefits, trade-offs, etc.
- Permits quality control of information chain performance.

Second-Generation Characteristics:
- Measurements are process oriented.

Figure 15.19   *Measurement (common to most successful data quality programs)*

Definition: The process of evaluating (quality) performance, comparing that performance with standards or goals, and acting on the difference.

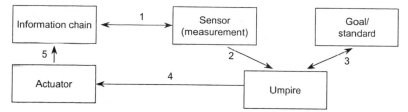

Motivation/Advantages:
- Predictability.
- Assures information chain performance to standard(s).

Second-Generation Characteristics:
- Heavy, though not exclusive, use of "statistical" process control.

Figure 15.20   *Quality control (common to most successful data quality programs)*

Definitions:

At the enterprise level: An annual process of setting quality goals or targets for quality levels and/or improvement and putting in place the means to achieve those goals.

At the "project" level: A team process that creates or replans new information products, information chains, or controls to meet specific customer needs.

Motivation/Advantages:
- Helps assure that information chains can consistently meet customer needs.

Second-Generation Characteristics:
- Structured methodology followed.
- Goals the responsibility of the quality council.
- Project teams chartered by quality council.

Note: We specifically include reengineering as a quality planning technique, implemented (only) when *major* changes are required.

Figure 15.21   *Quality planning (common to most successful data quality programs)*

Definition: A structured team process for reducing errors and other deficiencies in information chains and information products. It involves identifying and selecting improvement opportunities (projects), chartering teams to make improvements, completing those projects, and "holding the gains."

Motivation/Advantages:

- Experience suggests that improvement works best "project by project."
- Systematic process helps make improvement routine.
- Inculcation of "quality culture."

Second-Generation Characteristics:

- Discipline of working through quality council.
- Numerous projects.
- High rate of successful completion.

Figure 15.22   *Quality improvement (common to most successful data quality programs)*

Definition: The planned "blueprint" of an information chain, including suppliers, the sequence of work activities, interfaces, supporting technologies, management accountabilities, and information products delivered to customers.

Motivation/Advantages:

- New information chains are often needed to satisfy new customer needs.
- Redesign is an important component of reengineering.
- Well-planned and designed information chains perform better and faster and at lower total cost. They ease and speed development and implementation of supporting information technologies.

Second-Generation Characteristics:

- Designs promote data quality.
- Tools needed by the process owner (i.e., measurement and control) are built into the design.

Figure 15.23   *Information chain (re)design*

Definition: Evaluation of a quality specification for a collection of data (e.g., a checksum) and appropriate follow-up action. The follow-up may include: rejection of a collection, a process to find and correct defective data values, recording of results, etc.).

Motivation/Advantages:

- Prevents bad data from proceeding further into or through an information chain.

Second-Generation Characteristics:

- A relatively minor component of a good, second-generation system for data, but may be a critical component for complex information products.
- Edits built "in process," especially in data collection, data keying, etc.
- May also be employed as part of supplier program.
- Inspection results summarized and "out-of-control" situations identified and appropriate action taken.

Figure 15.24 *Inspection and test (data editing)*

Definitions:

At the enterprise level: Those activities that are designed to produce defect-free information products to meet the most important needs of the most important customers at the lowest possible cost.

At the operational level: Audits that determine the degree to which the Data Quality System, as designed, is being followed.

Motivation/Advantages:

- To provide management confidence that the organization is performing at optimal levels of effectiveness (meeting customer needs) and efficiency (minimal waste).
- To provide management confidence that control plans are being executed and that the quality system is deployed and functioning.
- To highlight areas for improvement.

Second-Generation Characteristics:

- All components of the data quality system personally approved and periodically reviewed by the data quality council.
- Audits institutionalized as part of the data quality system.
- Results of audits routinely appear on senior management's instrument panel for managing the business.

Figure 15.25 *Quality assurance*

Definition:

(1) Acts of reinforcement and feedback provided by senior management where:

- Information products and/or information chains have shown improvement.
- Information products and/or information chains have exceed expectations.
- Information products and/or information chains have consistently met standards over a period of time.
- Difficult assignments, such as improvement projects, have been successfully completed.

(2) A merit/compensation rating system that includes performance and activities required by the data quality system as part of periodic management reviews.

Motivation/Advantages:

- To continue to achieve improvements.
- To maintain enthusiasm and commitment to meeting customer needs.
- To help assure that standards are consistently met.
- To enhance the extent to which staff embrace the data quality system.

Second-Generation Characteristics:

- Periodic audits performed and feedback delivered personally by senior management.
- Appropriate positive feedback delivered personally by senior managers to project teams, functions, etc., as earned.
- Compensation increases and promotion decisions take employees' contributions to the data quality system into account.

Figure 15.26   *Rewards and Recognition*

Definition: Procedures to control documents and data/information that relate to requirements of the data quality system. Includes a master list of control procedures to identify the current version of policies, procedures, results, etc.

Motivation/Advantages:

* To mitigate the use of nonapplicable data policies, procedures, documents, standards, etc.

Second-Generation Characteristics:

* Any change to data policies, procedures, information products, standards, etc., are automatically entered into the document control process.
* All users know about and have easy access to the "master file."

Figure 15.27   *Document assurance*

Definition: Clear perception by all involved of the enterprise's data and information assets (both in principle and practice), their characteristics, and how they add value to the enterprise.

Motivation/Advantages:

* Good quality systems always take advantage of "domain information."
* Data and information (and their more esoteric brethren, knowledge and wisdom) are elusive concepts, which need to be clarified and disseminated.
* They differ in some critical ways from other assets.

Second-Generation Characteristics:

* Solid and growing perception.

Figure 15.28   *Domain knowledge of data and information*

Definition:

A rule or basis of comparison. The rules are usually developed and
   agreed upon by a body with authority to do so. So the term is used:

- In a "global sense," as in the ISO 9000 series.
- In a "company-wide" sense, as in standard terminology or supplier
  programs.
- Narrowly, as in quality control.

Motivation/Advantages:

- Help make future performance predictable.
- Acceptance/rejection of an information product.

Second-Generation Characteristics:

- Standards chain well managed and voluntary.
- Compliance widespread, with a well-known and managed "exception"
  process.

Figure 15.29   *Standards*

Definition: A published "book" containing an enterprise's quality
   policy, important concepts and definitions, and procedures.
   Ideally the handbook is customized to the enterprise, specifically
   general for widespread use, yet specific enough to help focus
   the enterprise's efforts.

Motivation/Advantages:

- Codifies the quality system.
- Increases the "reach" of the quality council.
- Many enterprises become comfortable with the concepts
  through the creation of the handbook.

Second-Generation Characteristics:

- Describes second-generation policies, techniques, procedures.
- Widely distributed.
- Under constant review and kept current.

Figure 15.30   *Quality handbook*

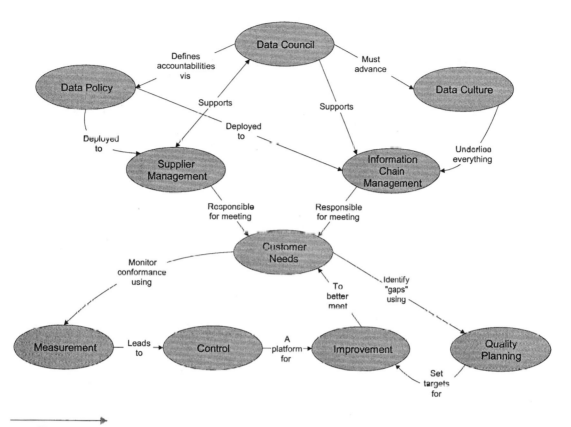

Figure 15.31 *The components of second-generation data quality systems reinforce one another*

16

The Customer-Supplier Model

Figure 16.1 depicts the so-called Customer-Supplier Model. Simple as the model appears, it is loaded with important features. The figure depicts three individuals and their work. The middle triangle represents the reader and his or her work. Information products that result from this work flow to customers on the right, who, in turn, use these information products to service customers, make decisions, plan, and produce further information products. To the left are suppliers. These are the people who produce the input (data and information products) the reader needs to do his or her work (center triangle).

Thus, the large arrows connecting the suppliers, the reader, and customers represent the flow of work and the creation of further information products. The triangles can also be thought of as three steps of an information chain.

The model makes clear that each person serves in three roles. The first role, completing his or her work, has already been discussed. The other two roles are made clear by shifting perspective. First, shift the perspective to that of the supplier, as depicted in Figure 16.2. The supplier sees the person to his or her right, in the original middle triangle, as the customer, the second role played by each person.

Conversely, shifting the triangles to the right yields the original customer's perspective. To the customer, the person in the original middle box is a supplier.

The triangles can be shifted to the left and right indefinitely. Doing so reveals that each person serves in three slightly different roles, with three slightly different main goals. To simplify somewhat:

- In completing their work, everyone must satisfy their support managers (bosses).

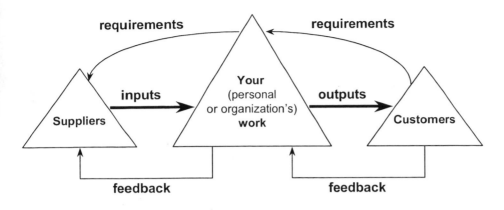

Figure 16.1   *Customer-supplier model*

- As suppliers, everyone must satisfy their customers.

- As customers, everyone wants to help make suppliers effective.

People (and organizations) play the three roles simultaneously. And for an end-to-end information chain to work well, they must be effective in each role.

Figure 16.2 features four other lines, depicting two requirements channels and two feedback channels. If a person is to provide high-quality data, he or she must understand customer requirements. Likewise, this person must receive feedback that enables him or her to compare performance against requirements. Similar requirements and feedback channels are needed with suppliers.

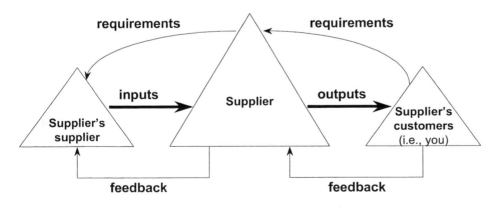

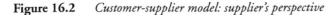

Figure 16.2   *Customer-supplier model: supplier's perspective*

The importance of these requirements and feedback channels cannot be overstated. Without them it is simply unrealistic to expect high-quality data. But these channels are absent (or clogged with noise, innuendo, and rumor) in too many cases. Like most consultants, I ask the same three questions over and over. Mine are: Who are the customers? What do they want? Are you meeting their needs?" I get a range of answers. The most depressing was "I haven't been yelled at this week, so I must be doing something right." Not very rich communications channnels.

The Year 2000 computer problem (millennium bug) was a direct result of the lack of such channels, according to one expert. Even though software developers were well aware of the problem and its potential impact at least 20 years in advance, they were not given clear requirements to prevent it or feedback that this offending feature was worth fixing.

Even more importantly, building requirements and feedback channels are the most effective steps to improve data quality. And it is usually easier than people think it will be. Most people want to both provide quality data and information products and need them from their suppliers. So in many cases it is a simple matter of putting the right people in a room together. Organizational barriers sometimes prevent this—a subject we'll consider in Chapter 33.

One final comment about the customer-supplier model: While it was presented from the point of view of the individual, the model is equally valid from the point of view of the organization, be that organization an entire company or a department within a company. Just as individuals have customers and suppliers, so too do departments and companies. And just as individuals must create requirements and feedback channels, so too must departments and companies.

Field Tip 16.1: To improve quality, first implement effective requirements and feedback channels with customers and suppliers.

E

Blocking and Tackling

There are certain technical skills that are absolutely essential if an organization is to effectively manage and improve data quality. These include the following:

- *Understanding customer needs (Chapter 17). After all, if customers are the final arbiters of quality, it pays to understand what they want.*

- *Measurement of actual quality levels against requirements (Chapters 18 and 19).*

- *Controls (gasp!) to keep errors from leaking through to customers (Chapter 20).*

- *Statistical control (double gasp!!) to make future performance predictable. In particular, to know that future errors will be prevented (Chapter 21).*

- *Quality improvement to close the most important gaps between actual and required performance (Chapter 22).*

- *Quality planning to set targets for improvement and to design new information chains (Chapters 23 and 24).*

Five of these tasks are among the ten elements of successful second-generation data quality systems.

This section describes how these tasks are accomplished. As noted, they are the essential skills of data quality management and improvement, and organizations must do them tolerably well. Section F presents structured approaches for organizing sequences of these activities. In particular, the trick is not to complete one quality improvement project (although you can't complete a second until you've completed a first), but to complete them routinely and continuously on data that produce the biggest benefit for the organization.

A final chapter describes relationships between quality improvement and re-engineering (Chapter 25).

17

Understanding Customer Needs (After All, They Are the Final Arbiters of Quality)

Establishing the requirements channel, as called for in the customer-supplier model, is not as simple as sending an e-mail request to the customer and receiving complete, current, requirements by return e-mail. There are at least four complicating factors, none admitting a simple solution, as follows:

1. Customers don't know what they want. And they don't have enough knowledge to provide real help. Customers have only superficial understanding of their requirements at best. They can opine that they "want timely, accurate data," but little else.

2. At the same time, customers can have a stunning array of needs. Beyond the usual "timely, accurate data," customers almost always want:

   - Data that are directly relevant to the task at hand
   - Clear, intuitive definitions of records, fields, values, and so on
   - The "right" level of detail
   - A comprehensive set of data (to complete the task at hand)
   - Data to be presented in easy-to-understand formats
   - Easy access to needed data
   - Low cost
   - Data about themselves to be kept private
   - To see the biggest "gaps" between what they currently receive and what they really need closed

3. There are many customers with different needs. Some needs even conflict.

4. Customer needs change all the time. What was good enough one day is simply not good enough the next.

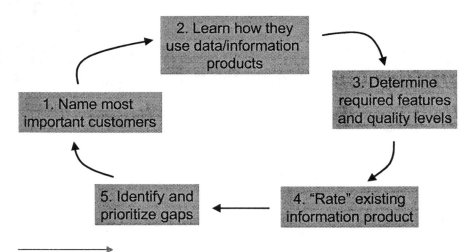

Figure 17.1   *Customer needs chain*

Faced with these realities, what exactly should one do? The next several paragraphs present one approach that has been field tested to positive reviews. It is neither easy nor fast. Nor does it require specialized skills, other than the abilities to listen, to organize what has been heard, to translate subjective opinion into objective requirements, and to make (a few) tough choices.

The customer needs chain is presented from the point of view of the data supplier, though with suitable modifications the chain can be led by the data customer. Such a data customer may wish to communicate formal requirements to a critical supplier.

The customer needs chain is summarized in Figure 17.1 and described in more detail in Figure 17.2. Figure 17.3 presents a generic customer needs spreadsheet for organizing information developed in the various steps of the chain. One feature of the customer needs spreadsheet is the columns labeled "Dimensions . . .". Table 17.1 provides a long list of dimensions of data quality. Those that customers cite most often are followed by an asterisk and defined in the glossary.

The customer needs chain is long and difficult. Unfortunately, there is no silver bullet. At least the chain does address the four issues raised above. First, it recognizes that, while customers don't know what they want, most can describe how they use data—the decisions they must make, the operations they must conduct, and so forth. Thus, customers have needs of the form "I need to complete such and such a task." The portion of the analysis conducted with customers will concentrate on understanding these needs.

Step 2
A. Make necessary plans.
B. Ask selected customers how they use information products. State in terms of "needs," (e.g., "need to complete this operation," "need to make that decision," etc.)
C. Organize on customer needs spreadsheet.
D. If greater detail is needed, identify "secondary needs," etc.
E. Prioritize customer needs.
F. Translate into technical language.
G. Review with selected customers and modify as needed.

Step 3
A. For each customer need, state the requirement associated with each quality dimension. Organize on spreadsheet. Add dimensions if appropriate.
B. Review requirements to ensure that, taken together, they will meet the customer need (if met). Modify as needed.
C. Review with selected customers. Modify as needed.
D. Summarize most stringent customer requirements.
E. Prioritize requirements.

Step 4
A. For each requirement (or the priority requirements), "rate" current performance.
To do so
• ask selected customers
• make measurements (Chapter 18)
• ask those who create the product
B. Organize on customer needs spreadsheet.

Step 1
A. List internal customers.
B. List external customers.
C. Prioritize both lists.

Step 5
A. Note gaps.
B. Develop priority list.
C. Review with selected customers and modify as needed.

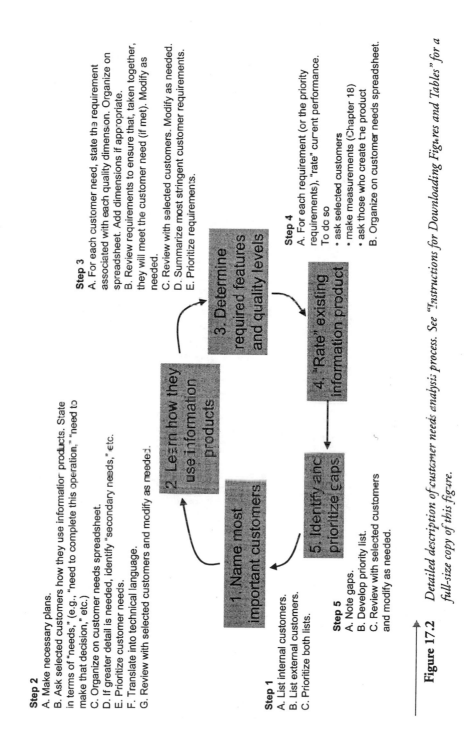

Figure 17.2 *Detailed description of customer needs analysis process. See "Instructions for Downloading Figures and Tables" for a full-size copy of this figure.*

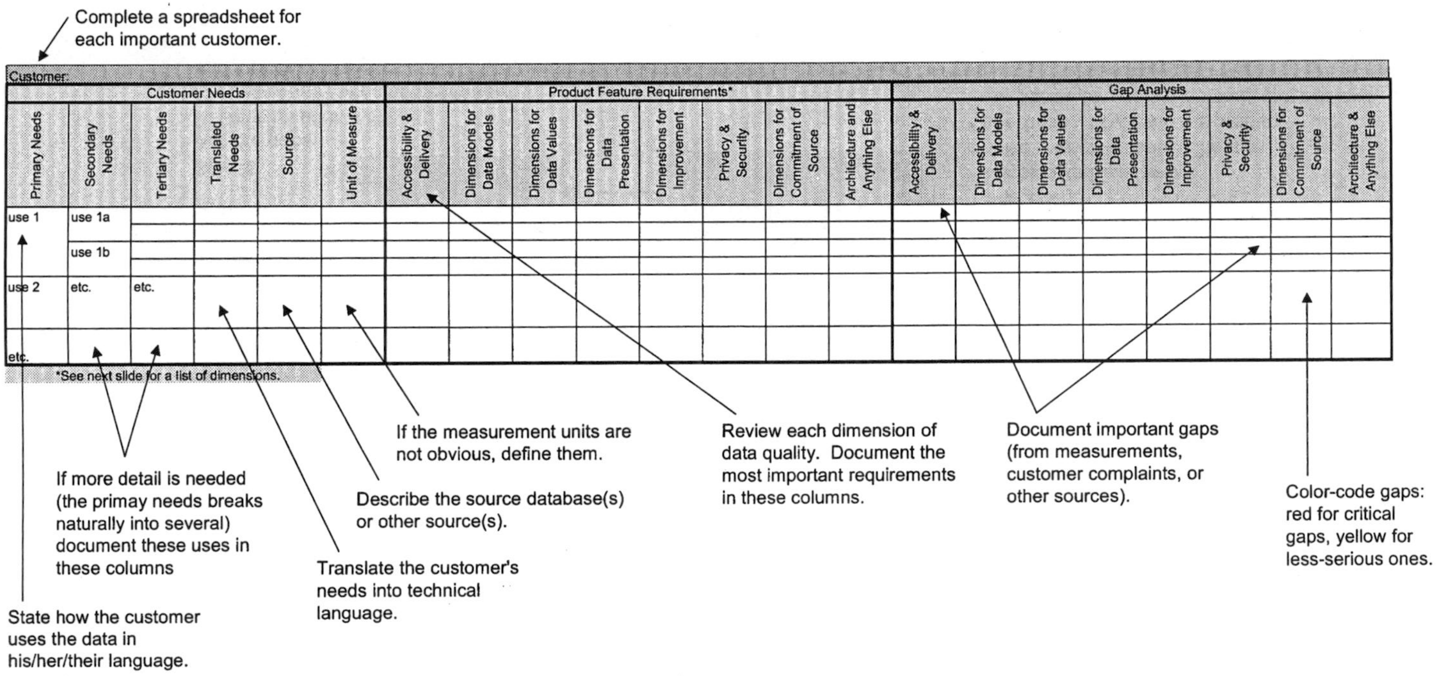

Figure 17.3 *Customer needs spreadsheet. See "Instructions for Downloading Figures and Tables" for a full-size copy of this figure.*

The supplier will have to figure out data requirements (or "customer wants") to meet these needs.

Second, it recognizes the stunning array of potential customer requirements and provides a checklist for developing a complete list. Naturally, some dimensions are more common than others. The most common are followed by an asterisk in Table 17.1. Importantly, many of these dimensions do not even bear on data directly. For example, the requirement that "data be kept safe from unauthorized access," is pertinent to supporting information technology, not data. Most customers do not make any kind of distinction between data and information technology, since in their eyes the two are so tightly coupled.

Third, it recognizes that a data supplier cannot meet all needs of all customers. The supplier must make choices. Fortunately, not all customers are created equal, some are simply more important than others. Further, not all needs are created equal. Thus, as a practical matter, quality involves "meeting the most important needs of the most important customers." Customer needs analysis strives to make good choices.

Finally, it recognizes how fast needs change and it allots time for understanding customer needs on an ongoing basis. It recognizes that data suppliers, with more intimate knowledge of their data than customers, may be able to suggest new data products and simpler ways for customers to do their work.

Field Tip 17.1: Determining customer needs is unbelievably hard work. But there is no substitute for doing so. And the rewards are great.

Field Tip 17.2: As a practical matter, data quality involves meeting the most important needs of the most important customers. Be prepared to make the tough choices.

Field Tip 17.3: You can't reasonably expect data customers to develop detailed requirements. Instead, work with them to figure out how they use data and their needs. Data sources must translate those needs into requirements.

Table 17.1　　*Complete List of Dimensions of Data Quality*

Category/Dimension	Category/Dimension
Accessibility/Delivery	*Presentation Quality*
Availability*	Appropriateness
Protocol	Format Precision
Security*	Use of Storage
Quality of Content	*Flexibility*
Attribute Granularity	Portability
Comprehensiveness*	Representation Consistency
Essentialness	Null Values
Flexibility	Formats
Appropriate Use*	Language
Areas Covered	Ease of Interpretation*
Homogeneity	*Improvement*
Naturalness	Feedback
Obtainability	Measurement*
Precision of Domains	Track Record
Robustness	*Privacy*
Semantic Consistency	Consumer Privacy
Structural Consistency	Privacy of Others
Simplicity	Security
Clear Definition*	*Commitment*
Identifiability**	Early Warning*
Source*	Help*
Relevancy*	Special Requests
Quality of Values	Commitment
Accuracy*	*Architecture*
Completeness	Library/Documentation*
Timeliness	Logical Structure
Consistency	Physical Structure
	Naming*
	Rules
	Redundancy
	Unit Cost*

*Often the dimensions the data customers most often cite, though not always using these terms.

**A critical dimension that data customers often forget, but is usually of critical importance to them.

18

Better, Faster, Cheaper

The title for this chapter stems from the simple observation that, diverse as customers are, most simply want the data to be better, they want them faster, and they want them cheaper. Customer needs and the requirements that result are subjective. The question of whether they are met, absent hard measurements against them, can dissolve into unproductive chatter based on anecdotes, excuses, long-held opinions, and pet agendas. Some customer complaints such as "These data are not relevant to my needs," are cut and dried. The more subjective ones include "The data always come in too late," "There are too many missing values," and "These data have too many errors." And nothing gets better.

Measurements can help, as shown in the following list:

- Measurements replace anecdote with fact.
- Measurements inform management of the depth of a problem, allowing it to be meaningfully compared with other problems.
- Measurements help localize sources of important problems.
- Measurements confirm that solutions really work.
- Measurements help customers understand what they really get.

In summary, it seems that most organizations only manage what they measure.

Measurements yield great power to those who have them. Used properly, they provide enormous benefit. They may also be used improperly and cause great harm. Thus, measurements may reveal that the results delivered by an untrained clerk really are much poorer that those of the clerk's colleagues. And those who "pay for performance" may be inclined to terminate this employee. But the measurements may not reveal that the clerk was not properly trained to do the job and that the proper action is training, not termination.

Due to their enormous power and examples such as this one, measurements are a tender issue in many organizations. It can be a tough bind. On the one hand measurements are essential, on the other they can be misused.

The right measurements depend on the maturity of the organization's data quality program. Organizations just starting out do not need sophisticated, scientifically defensible measurements. They need simple measures that indicate where they are, the impact(s), and the first couple of opportunities for improvement. At a slightly more mature level, organizations need solid enough measurements to inform communications channels between themselves, customers, and suppliers and to effect process control (Chapter 21). Organizations with advanced data quality programs (and high-quality data) will require more sophisticated measurements, such as those obtained from data tracking (Chapter 19).

Even at the most basic level, there are many good ways to proceed. Here we describe one measurement chain that aims to answer the question "Is data quality an issue?" quickly. An overview of the chain is given in Figure 18.1 and more details are provided in Figures 18.2 and 18.3.

This simple measurement chain, like any other, must have customers. Organizations can waste a lot of time and effort taking measurements that no one will ever use. The question "Who is expected to do what with

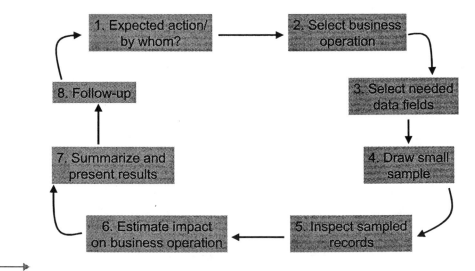

Figure 18.1   *"Is data quality an issue?" measurement chain*

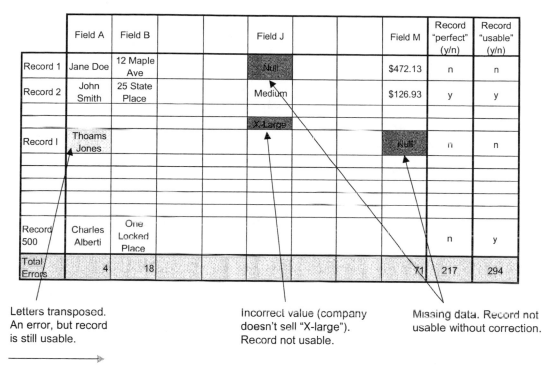

	Field A	Field B			Field J			Field M	Record "perfect" (y/n)	Record "usable" (y/n)
Record 1	Jane Doe	12 Maple Ave			Null			$472.13	n	n
Record 2	John Smith	25 State Place			Medium			$126.93	y	y
					X-Large					
Record I	Thoams Jones							Null	n	n
Record 500	Charles Alberti	One Locked Place							n	y
Total Errors	4	18						71	217	294

Letters transposed. An error, but record is still usable.

Incorrect value (company doesn't sell "X-large"). Record not usable.

Missing data. Record not usable without correction.

Figure 18.2   *Example of a simple spreadsheet for estimating error rates*

Summary error rates at the "record" and "field" levels:

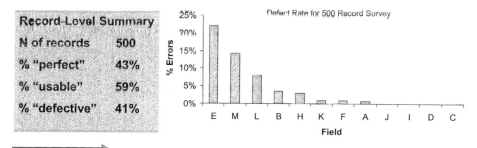

Record-Level Summary	
N of records	500
% "perfect"	43%
% "usable"	59%
% "defective"	41%

Defect Rate for 500 Record Survey

Figure 18.3   *Example top-line summary results of first measurements*

results?" should always be asked before measurement is seriously contemplated. The answer to "Is data quality an issue?" may be a clear-cut "No!" in which case no further action is indicated. But it is indeed unforgivable if the answer is "Yes," (as it more often is) and there is no follow-up. This *Field Guide* recognizes, and even encourages, "skunk works." A middle manager who suspects poor data lie at the root of an important business issue may decide to, rather quietly, make some simple measurements to find out. The manager must realize that he or she is the only customer and think through the next step. Importantly, thoughtful managers almost always accept compelling results. They make good customers for initial studies such as this one.

Second, selecting records directly from a database is sometimes inadequate. Even rather provocative results, such as "Fifty percent of the sampled records contained an error" can be met with responses of "So what?" This is why the first step of the measurement chain is selecting a business operation, downstream of the selected data. The impact of poor data on that business operation should be estimated.

Third, select the sample with some care. The most important factors are customer needs and simplicity. People may challenge results based on woeful samples. Be open and forthcoming about the sampling scheme.

Fourth, determine what it means for a record to be "seriously flawed" and perhaps "flawed but acceptable." Seriously flawed records are those that require rework before the downstream business operation can be completed. Flawed but acceptable records are those that are not perfect, but the downstream process can accommodate them easily. For example, if a customer's first name is actually "John" but appears in a database as "Jon," a customer service representative will still be able to talk to this customer.

Fifth, to estimate impact, ask people who work the downstream process. Ask about added time and expense (to correct errors), customer satisfaction, and impacts to decision making.

Finally, while data accuracy measurements are essential and a good place to start, they are not the only important measurements. Simple measurements of cycle time (i.e., faster), productivity or cost (cheaper), and customer satisfaction are also useful. The cycle time associated with an information chain is the time it takes to complete a unit of work. Both a start time and a stop time must be specified and it is usually best to specify those times from the customer's perspective. Thus, from the customer's perspective, in ordering merchandise from a direct mailer, he or she will consider the start time to be the moment the order is placed and the stop time to be the moment all ordered items arrive correctly. As with accuracy, a small, well-selected sample is a good place to begin.

This also applies to cost or productivity. Most accounting systems do not distinguish between value-added work and non–value-added work to find and correct errors. But downstream departments (and customers) may bear significant costs as a result of upstream errors. Thus, in estimating unit cost or productivity, it is important that all costs, not just those incurred within a given department, be included. This is extremely important from a data quality perspective, because the department creating errors may bear some investment expense to implement its data quality system. Downstream departments should feel relief in short order.

Field Tip 18.1: Before taking measurements of data quality levels, first think through how the customers of the results should use them.

Field Tip 18.2: Present results in simple, compelling formats. Emphasize not just the error rate, but the impact on the organization.

Field Tip 18.3: Use examples to illustrate results. But do not confuse an anecdote with a compelling case for action.

19

Measurement 2: Data Tracking

The simple measurement procedure described in Chapter 18 is more than adequate for obtaining initial estimates of data quality levels. And it is useful for confirming that improvements have been sustained. But it does not always provide the depth needed to determine where errors occur. Nor does it provide direct measurements of cycle time. In those situations where more detailed in-line measurements[1] are needed, data tracking is the measurement vehicle of choice.

When one tracks, one follows something from beginning to end. When one tracks data, one follows the data from their birth, through the various steps in information chains that manipulate the data. One also time-stamps the various steps or events as they occur. The simple, hypothetical information chain shown in Figure 19.1 is sufficient to illustrate the main points. The chain is designed to satisfy some customer need. Four departments are involved in doing so and a data record is updated as work is completed. Eventually the work is complete and a data record is stored in a database for later use.

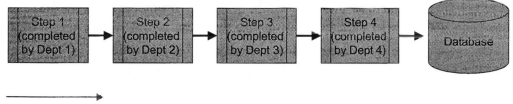

Figure 19.1   *Simple information chain to illustrate data tracking*

---

1.   An "in-chain" or "in-line" measurement is one that is made inside an information chain, in contrast to a static measurement, which is made of data already-created and stored in a database.

Translation change: "157-238" and John Smith are the same person, but few without training would guess it.

Operations change: Digits are transposed and these codes do not represent the same items.

data field	Step 1	Step 2	Step 3	Step 4	Database
		Step in Information Chain			
Name	157-238	John Smith	John Smith	John Smith	John Smith
Credit	NA	ok	no	no	no
Item	150-678-B	150-678-B	150-768-B	150-768-B	150-768-B
Size	large	large	L	L	L
Ship date	Friday, Sept 16, 2000	15-Sep-00	15-Sep-00	15-Sep-00	15-Sep-00
Start Date/Time	9:00 AM, Monday, Sept 11, 2000	4:00 PM, Monday, Sept 11, 2000	11:00 AM, Wednesday, Sept 13, 2000	2:05 PM, Thursday, Sept 14, 2000	3:00 PM, Thursday, Sept 14, 2000
Complete Date/Time	9:30 AM, Monday, Sept 11, 2000	4:20 PM, Monday, Sept 11, 2000	11:15 AM, Wednesday, Sept 13, 2000	3:00 PM, Thursday, Sept 14, 2000	NA

Error: Sept. 16, 2000 is not a Friday.

Normalization change: "large" and "L" mean the same thing, and the change is easily recognized.

Figure 19.2 *Example tracked record*

Figure 19.2 gives a simple example of a tracked record for five important fields and the times at which work on each step was started and stopped. Essentially the table contains the contents of the selected fields at each step along the way. The time stamps detail critical times as the work unit and data record wind their way through the chain.

The figure illustrates four changes or errors to data fields:

1. A normalization change: Such changes are the result of different format requirements of underlying computer systems. But the eye easily recognizes that the information content is the same.

2. A translation change: Such changes also do not change the information content, but the untrained human cannot easily confirm this. Such changes may result because the departments conducting the work have different technical requirements.

3. An operations change (or error): These changes result because one department doubts the work performed at a previous step and changes the data value.

4. An error: Detected by applying the business rules (see Chapter 20) to data at their first points of entry.

Technically, normalization and translation changes are not errors. They may occasionally add value to the information chain because they make it easier for some work to be completed. But most often they simply add unneeded complication. So the focus should be on errors (including operations changes). Operations changes do not conclusively indicate which person, organization, or step made an error. For the operations change depicted in Figure 19.2 there are three possibilities:

1. A correct data field was made incorrect at step 3.

2. An incorrect field was corrected at step 3.

3. An incorrect field was changed incorrectly at step 3.

Importantly, the spirit of quality improvement is not to fix blame, but rather to fix the problem. Any of the three eventualities indicate a problem on the interface between steps 2 and 3 (most data errors stem from a lack of communications between departments). Information chain management is ideal for building the needed communications channels and eliminating the resultant data errors. (See Chapter 27.)

The start and stop times are used to calculate cycle time. The particular record of Figure 19.2 took a total of 3 days, six hours to wind its way from the start of the chain into the storage database. Note that there is a great deal of time from the completion of one step until the start of the next. This usually represents queue or wait time. Nothing is happening to the record (more importantly to the work it represents). It is just in a wait state. For this record, the first step took half an hour to complete, the second 20 minutes, the third step 15 minutes, and the fourth and final step took 55 minutes. Thus:

- Total work time = 2 hours

- Total non-work time = 28 hours

- Total end-to-end time = 30 hours

If cycle time is an issue, one is well-advised to focus on reducing the non-work time. Not only is the potential reduction larger, it is usually easier to make.

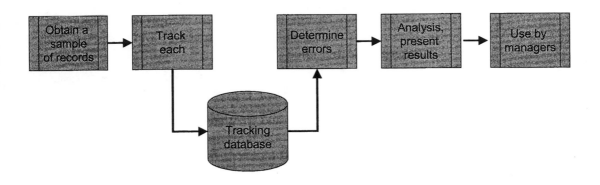

Figure 19.3   *Data tracking chain*

Figure 19.2 thus yields detailed information about what happened to this particular data record. It does not a useful measurement make. To create needed measurement summaries one completes the data tracking chain (pictured in Figure 19.3):

- Select a sample of records to track.

- Obtain the information of Figure 19.2 for each.

- Determine which changes represent errors.

- Analyze the errors and cycle time data, present results.

- Use results to establish control and/or make needed improvements.

The most important summaries of error rate results are provided by control charts (see Chapter 21) and histograms. Figure 19.4 is an example. The histogram resembles the Pareto charts of Chapter 18 (see Figure 18.3), with two critical differences. First, the x-axis is based on pairs of steps in the

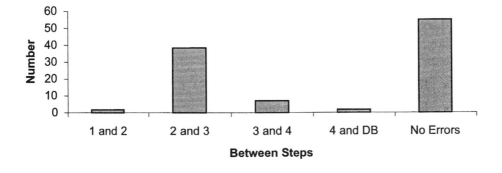

Figure 19.4   *Histogram of errors (100 tracked errors)*

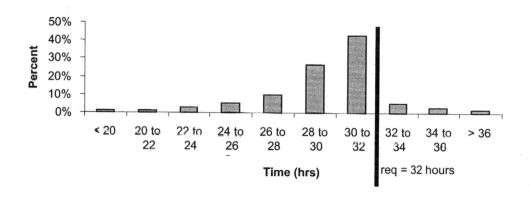

Figure 19.5   *Cycle time for 100 tracked records*

information chain (not data fields). Second, the order of the labels is determined by the sequence of these steps (not the error rate). The proper interpretation of Figure 19.4 is that most errors occur between steps 2 and 3 of the information chain.

A histogram also provides a useful summary of cycle time measurements. Figure 19.5 is an example. In this plot, we have assumed that the cycle time requirement is 4 days (or 32 hours). So the plot indicates that 5% of the work is completed beyond the requirement.

Another histogram, Figure 19.6, decomposes the value-added or work time and the non–value-added or queue time. In the single record example above, non–value-added time completely dominates value-added time. So too for the entire sample.

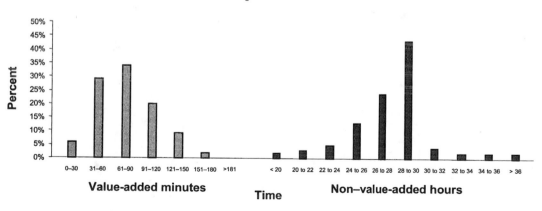

Figure 19.6   *Value-added/non–valued-added time (100 tracked records)*

Field Tip 19.1: Data tracking is the measurement vehicle of choice when detailed, in-chain measurements of data accuracy and cycle time are needed.

20

Edit Controls

By definition (Figure 15.19), "control" is "the managerial act of measuring performance, comparing performance against standards, and acting on the difference" (Joseph Juran). Most people are familiar with many types of controls. A thermostat effects control. The thermostat's thermometer detects room temperature more or less continuously. If it gets too cold, the thermostat turns on the furnace. When the room warms up, it turns the furnace off. Similarly, budgetary controls compare actual expenditures against planned expenditures and warn managers that they must take appropriate actions.

For data quality, one simple type of control is called an "edit control." Statistical controls are discussed in Chapter 21. Edit controls involve business rules based on the domains of data values permitted for a given field, pair of fields, and so on. Thus, for a person's address, the combination AREA CODE = 212 (New York City) and ZIP CODE = 90210 (Los Angeles, CA) should not be allowed.

Business rules apply to almost all data. The simplest are the so-called "univariate" (one variable) domains, which apply to a single field. Thus, the following all limit possible entries in the ZIP CODE field:

- ZIP CODE is a required field.

- ZIP CODEs must have five digits.

- ZIP CODEs must appear in the Postal Standard.

Bivariate domains are those that involve two fields. The ZIP and AREA CODES are a common example. Trivariate domains are those that involve three, and so forth. Business rules can be quite complex.

The process (see Figure 20.1) for creating and applying edits is as follows:

1.   Specify the domains of allowed values.

2.   Translate them into business rules.

3.   Apply them to the data.

4.   For each rule, list all records that fail.

Ideally, domains of allowed values and business rules are developed within the data modeling chain (see Chapter 5), though often they must be "rediscovered" later. In almost all cases, rules may be computerized (some software products even help discover the domains). Finally, for editing to meet the definition of "control," appropriate management action is required. Usually that management action involves some form of correction, the most difficult step in most organizations.

Data editing cannot be the heart and soul of a data quality program because, in and of itself, it does not prevent future errors. But used properly, it can be an important contributor. The following text summarizes how data edits may be used.

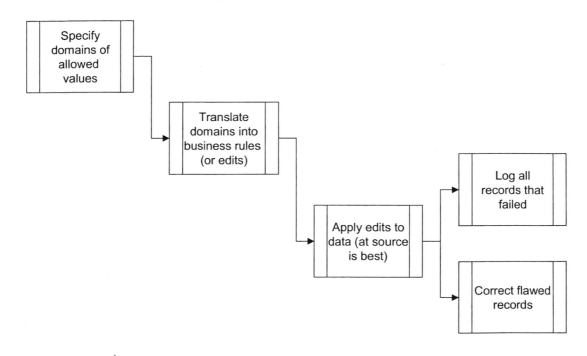

Figure 20.1   *Development and use of edit controls*

First, the principles of data editing are exactly those of data clean-up, so editing can be applied to an existing database. Absent a program to ensure that newly created data values are of high quality, this is usually a bad idea. Second, edits can be applied as input criteria to a database. Flawed data are simply not allowed. Third, and even further upstream, edits can be applied as people enter data. They can immediately be prompted to make corrections. Application of edits in this way is called "in-chain editing," and it can work well.

But, as noted previously, data editing cannot be the heart and soul of a data quality program. Even in-chain editing has several shortcomings, including the following:

- It leads to a false sense of security that data are correct. But being correct and being within the allowed domain are two different things.

- Within an information chain, most operators soon learn how to "fool the system." They learn that "12 Main Street, Anytown, USA" is a valid address and, absent the correct address, use it to bypass the edits.

- Editing takes a lot of time and costs a lot of money. The most time-consuming and expensive step involves correcting the errors. Except in special circumstances, this is labor-intensive.

- The edits themselves require a lot of maintenance. Domains change and new data fields are developed all the time.

- Finally, and most importantly, edits do not prevent future errors.

Field Tip 20.1: Just because data have passed the edits, does not ensure that the data are of acceptable quality.

Field Tip 20.2: Data editing should be employed (as part of a larger data quality program) to prevent errors from causing damage downstream.

21

Statistical Control: Establishing a Basis for Prediction

The paradigm of prevention requires the organization to think not so much about the past as about the future. Questions such as: "What is going to happen next week?" and "Will customer needs be met next week?" are more important than their historical counterparts: "What happened last week?" and "Were customer needs met last week?"

The distinction is both profound and subtle.

This chapter provides a simple means for answering the first two questions. Statistical Process Control provides the required basis. (In the United States, the words "statistics" and "control" often have negative connotations. People are afraid of statistics and dislike being controlled.) It was invented in the 1920s by Walter Shewhart to improve manufacture of telecommunications equipment and has enjoyed unparalleled success in thousands of settings. It has proven successful in data quality as well. The reader interested in further descriptions of the mathematical foundations of quality control should consult E. L. Grant and R. S. Leavenworth, *Statistical Quality Control*, 6th ed. (New York: McGraw-Hill, 1988).

Figures 21.1 and 21.2 are example time series plots of error rates, such as obtained from the measurement process described in Chapters 18 and 19. Three additional lines have been added to the plot, a center line, an upper control limit, and a lower control limit.

Few people would be comfortable making any prediction based on Figure 21.1. There is simply too much variation. In the lingo of Statistical Process Control (SPC), the plot indicates an out-of-control or unstable situation. The cause(s) of this instability must be found and eliminated.

Figure 21.2 presents a different situation. Of course, there is still variation, but not too much. Most of the points concentrate around the center line and none exceeds the control limits. Predictions such as "We expect next week's performance to be about the center line, and we'll be very

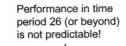

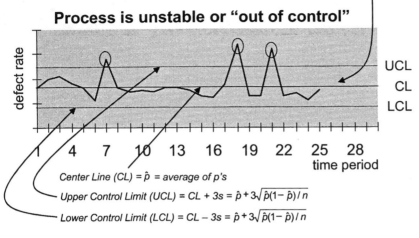

Process is unstable or "out of control"

defect rate

1   4   7   10   13   16   19   22   25   28
                                    time period

Center Line (CL) = $\hat{p}$ = average of p's

Upper Control Limit (UCL) = CL + 3s = $\hat{p} + 3\sqrt{\hat{p}(1-\hat{p})/n}$

Lower Control Limit (LCL) = CL − 3s = $\hat{p} + 3\sqrt{\hat{p}(1-\hat{p})/n}$

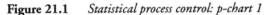

Figure 21.1   *Statistical process control: p-chart 1*

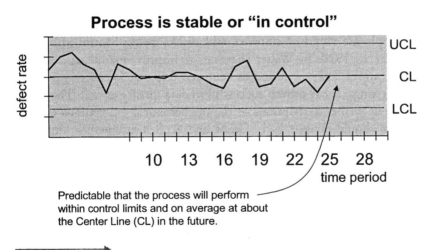

Process is stable or "in control"

defect rate

10   13   16   19   22   25   28
                          time period

Predictable that the process will perform
within control limits and on average at about
the Center Line (CL) in the future.

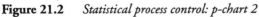

Figure 21.2   *Statistical process control: p-chart 2*

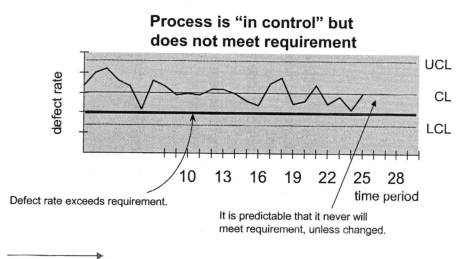

Figure 21.3   *It is meaningful to compare the performance of a stable process with requirements*

surprised if it falls outside the control limits" are justified. Further, if next week's performance does exceed control limits, then something very unusual (an instability) has occurred. And the data quality manager should find and eliminate it as soon as possible.

Of course, predictable does not mean "good." Thus, in Figure 21.3 a "customer requirements line" has been added to Figure 21.2. It is clear that next week's predicted error rate will far exceed customer requirements. In other words, it is predictable that customer requirements will not be met next week (or any week in the future, for that matter). The process must be changed. Improvement projects, discussed in Chapter 22, are required.

Figure 21.4 summarizes the steps in constructing and interpreting p-charts, and Figure 21.5 summarizes the logic in flowchart form. It is rare that an existing information chain is either in control or meets customer needs when it is first addressed. The information chain or data supplier manager should first establish control by finding and eliminating sources of instability and then improving the underlying process so it meets customer needs. The goal is to create a control chart similar to that shown in Figure 21.6.

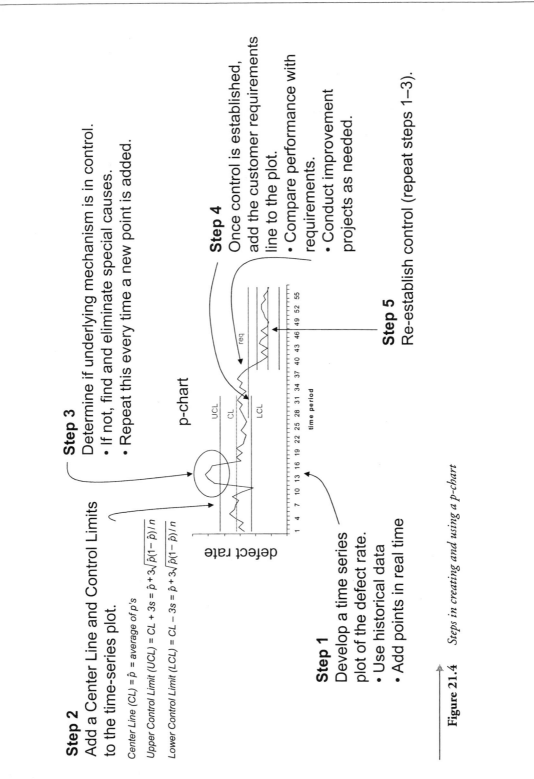

Step 2
Add a Center Line and Control Limits to the time-series plot.

Center Line (CL) = $\hat{p}$ = average of p's

Upper Control Limit (UCL) = CL + 3s = $\hat{p}$ + 3$\sqrt{\hat{p}(1-\hat{p})/n}$

Lower Control Limit (LCL) = CL − 3s = $\hat{p}$ + 3$\sqrt{\hat{p}(1-\hat{p})/n}$

Step 3
Determine if underlying mechanism is in control.
• If not, find and eliminate special causes.
• Repeat this every time a new point is added.

Step 4
Once control is established, add the customer requirements line to the plot.
• Compare performance with requirements.
• Conduct improvement projects as needed.

Step 5
Re-establish control (repeat steps 1–3).

Step 1
Develop a time series plot of the defect rate.
• Use historical data
• Add points in real time

p-chart

defect rate

time period

Figure 21.4   *Steps in creating and using a p-chart*

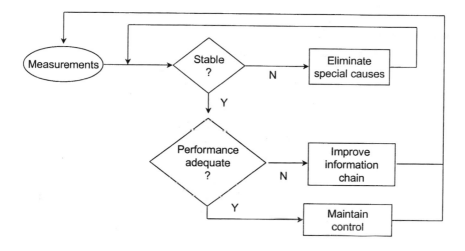

Figure 21.5 *Process controls: management activities to effect control and conformance to requirements*

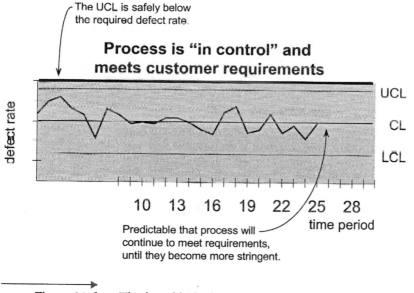

Figure 21.6 *The desired look of a control chart*

Record-level error rates from a sample of 500
orders are plotted every week on a p-chart.

Process goes out of control at time period 24.

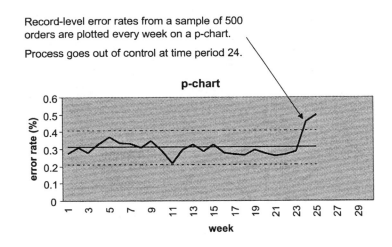

Figure 21.7   *Example: An out-of-control situation is detected*

Once control has been established, the manager must be vigilant to
ensure that it is maintained. Figures 21.7, 21.8, and 21.9 illustrate a frequent occurrence. In this example, a new software package is implemented.
As with most software, this package is not defect-free. Fortunately the information chain manager is able to detect the out-of-control situation immediately. While initially the manager may not know that the software package
is to blame, he or she is at least alerted to a special cause. A simple investigation reveals the root cause and the offending software is debugged.

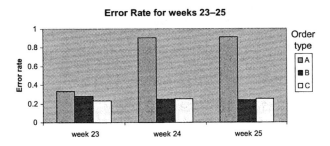

Reveals that the error rate for Order Type A dramatically
increases beginning in week 24.

Investigation suggests that new order processing software
was loaded in week 24.

It is the suspected culprit.

Figure 21.8   *The search for the special cause*

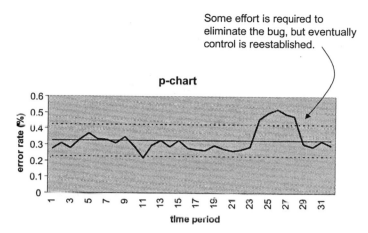

Figure 21.9   *Reestablishing control*

Field Tip 21.1: Use control charts to establish a technical basis for preventing errors. First establish control. Then make improvements to meet customer requirements.

22

Quality Improvement: Root Cause Analysis to Uncover the Real Causes of Error

A stable (in-control) information chain that does not meet customer needs must be changed. Data quality improvement is a structured method for doing so. The data quality improvement cycle is depicted in Figure 22.1 and practical tips for completing projects are given in Figure 22.2. It calls for a structured approach featuring well-defined projects, conducted by small, usually cross-functional teams. The structure is needed so that improvement projects can be started continually and successfully completed with high probability. While each project may be small, the cumulative impact is quite large. This *Field Guide* recommends a portfolio of improvement projects, most small and relatively easy to complete, a few larger ones, and an occasional demanding project. The more demanding projects should be undertaken only after the organization gains some experience with quality improvement.

The concept of reengineering is frequently set in contrast to data quality improvement (Chapter 25). Indeed, in some respects, reengineering is the large-scale version of data quality improvement. Reengineering aims for quantum improvements by considering all aspects of large information chains and potential new roles for information technology. Importantly, deciding whether to initiate a sequence of data quality improvement projects or to reengineer is rarely a tough choice. Even under the best of circumstances (the best people, all needed resources, and senior leadership), reengineering is a risky venture. Upwards of three-quarters of reengineering efforts fail. So it should only be considered when there is no other choice.

As noted, data quality improvement proceeds incrementally. The philosophy of continual improvement underlies almost all successful data quality programs. Even reengineered chains do not emerge in perfect functioning order from the design team, so they too must be improved. One other distinction between reengineering and data quality improvement is that it is possible for data quality improvement to be part of everyone's work. Most

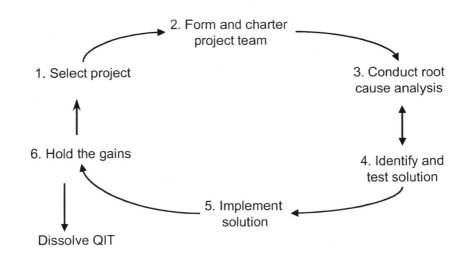

Figure 22.1   *Data quality improvement cycle (QIT)*

projects should require only a few hours of work per week and should be accommodated within people's day-in and day-out responsibilities.

For data, there are almost always plenty of opportunities for cream-skimming. This means that there are numerous projects, just waiting to be defined, that can be completed with relative ease. As with anything else in data, organizational politics may hinder quality improvement. The management structures defined in subsequent chapters help mitigate these hindrances. The following illustrates one such opportunity. It begins with the simple measurement results of Figure 18.4. For the sake of the example, we'll assume that an information chain owner has obtained these results. (We'll discuss the relationships between data quality improvement teams and other management structures in Chapters 26 and 27.) Based on these summaries, the owner decides to address field E (step 1).

So the owner begins work on the next step of the data quality improvement cycle. Specifically, the owner does the following:

- Forms a data quality improvement project team composed of one person from each major step of the information chain producing these records

- Selects a young woman to lead the team (in this case, part of the reason for this selection was to help her learn more about other organizations)

Step 1: Identifying and selecting projects
A. Solicit recommendations from customers, requirements that haven't been met, and supplier recommendations. Keep a list.
B. Select projects that balance:
  • The most important customer needs
  • Ease of completing the project ("cream skimming")"
  • Special interests
C. Remember that the goal is to complete (not start) projects. Set a reasonable goal, like "complete three projects per quarter."
D. Once a project has been selected, add it to the "project log." Distinguish "projects" from simple action items. Log action items as well.

Step 6: Hold the gains
A. With controls and information technology in place, the problem should not recur. The improvement project team is accountable to confirm this for one or two cycles.
B. Afterwards, the responsible manager should confirm from time to time.
C. To complete the project, make sure the project status report is complete.

Last, dissolve the project team
A. "Projects" should have definitive completions.
B. When the project team has completed its work, the team should be disbanded.
C. A small celebration is usually in order.

Step 2: Forming and chartering a project team
A. Name a project leader. Get the right people on the team.
B. Clearly articulate the project's charter, including:
  • The problem. Quantify where possible.
  • The impact of the problem (who, what, etc.).
  • What is expected (i.e., cut the error rate in the Irish market in half every three months). Quantify expected results.
  • Recognize that some projects will require resources.
C. Track progress every couple of weeks.
D. The project leader must keep the project status report up-to-date as progress is made.

Step 3: Conducting a root cause analysis
A. Find the root causes(s) of the problem. This is much like detective work.
B. Most often, people close to the problem know about it and why it occurs.
C. In many cases it is easier to split the problem into smaller problems. Example: The source of the problem in London is XYZ. In Frankfurt, it is ABC.

Step 4: Identify and trial solutions
A. Identify possible "full" and "partial" solutions. Two simple solutions that solve 90% of the problem are preferred to a complex solution that solves 95%.
B. Avoid solutions that "automate a "broken process."
C. Focus on "prevention." Resist clean-up until new data are of acceptable quality.
D. Put the solution as close to the problem as possible (if the root cause is in London, search for a solution there).
E. Where possible, conduct a small prototype of the solution. Select a simple geography, a subset of the data, or similar.
F. Prototypes should focus on "the process," usually of raw data collection. If the prototype works well, use information technology to automate the process (steps 5 and 6).

Step 5: Implement solution
A. Roll the solution out fully once it has proven itself.
B. Use the success on the prototype to build support.
C. In most cases, it is appropriate to implement a control to guarantee the solution.
D. Ensure that the solution will work in ongoing operations. Establishing clear management accountability for the ongoing solution is the first priority.
E. Use information technology to "lock in the gains."
F. Many improvement projects will involve increased understanding among the people involved. Ensuring continuity as people come and go can be especially difficult.

Figure 22.2   *Practical tips for completing improvement projects. For a full-size copy of this figure, see "Instructions for Downloading Figures and Tables."*

The owner and improvement team agree to the following charter (completing step 2):

Reduce the error rate in field E by 50 percent in three months. Reduce it by a further 50 percent (75 percent total) in three more. The improvement team agrees to provide a monthly status report to the owner.

The improvement team decides to meet weekly. Its first step is to develop an understanding of those aspects of the information chain that impact field E. The team learns that field E is added to the data record by clerks in the credit department. Five clerks perform this work and it is often considered, though not formally, an entry-level job.

The young woman meets with these clerks. One man admits that "He never knew what field E was for." So he just entered anything that the "system" would allow (see Chapter 20 for more on edit controls).

Further investigation reveals that the credit department's procedures did not specify how field E was to be populated and that the support manager assumed that "People who needed help got it from one another or from the support manager" (this completes step 3, root cause analysis).

One clerk agreed to explain the proper procedure to the man and he agreed to follow it (steps 4 and 5). The improvement team conducted a follow-up study of 100 records two weeks later (see Figure 22.3). Results confirmed the problem was solved (completing step 5).

A series of meetings with clerks and the support manager were held to discuss the best ways to address field C going forward. A number of simple ideas were presented. Several were selected and integrated together. Finally, all clerks agreed to follow an agreed-upon procedure (repeating steps 4 and 5). The support manager agreed to write the new procedure into the credit department's book of procedures. The manager also agreed to make sure new clerks were properly trained (step 6, holding the gains).

The improvement team, which had dutifully reported its work monthly to the process team, now reports that its work is complete. The entire project took three months (of the allotted six) and reduced the error rate by 81 percent (exceeding its target of 75 percent). The data quality improvement team was disbanded with the information chain owner's thanks.

There are two important points regarding this project. The first is that many projects really are this simple and beneficial. Seek them out early on. The second point is that the lack of a communications channel and poor training were at the root of many such simple opportunities. The clerk simply did not know what was expected and had not been properly trained.

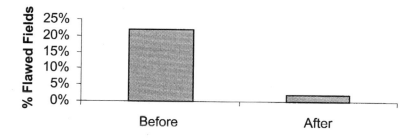

Figure 22.3   *Results of improvement project*

Many organizations are quick to blame the poor motivation of low-paid data entry clerks for their data quality woes. But, while people (including data entry clerks) do make mistakes, the fault for the vast majority of errors lies not with them, but with poor training, missing or confusing requirements, a rewards system that overemphasizes speed, or other similar factors.

Field Tip 22.1: Don't underestimate the simple elegance of data quality improvement. Other than teamwork, training, and discipline, it requires no special skills. Anyone who wants to can be an effective contributor.

Field Tip 22.2: Get in the habit of continuous improvement. Set and meet simple goals, such as "complete a project every month."

Field Tip 22.3: Carefully define most projects to be small and achievable by a small team of people in a short amount of time.

Field Tip 22.4: Poor training and/or communication of requirements lie at the root of many data quality problems. They are relatively easy to fix.

23

Quality Planning—Setting Targets for Improvement

We use the term "quality planning" in three contexts in this book:

1. For setting targets for improved quality

2. For designing new information chains

3. For integrating data quality and overall business strategy

This chapter discusses setting targets, and Chapter 24 discusses the design of new information chains. The essential issues regarding the linkage of data quality and overall business strategy were discussed in Chapters 7, 8, and 9.

This book recommends simple, easy-to-quantify targets that are explicitly linked to important business problems/opportunities. Thus, it recommends targets of the form:

Cut the percentage of new unacceptable records in half every six months for the next two years. In total, cut the error rate by 94 percent. Here, a record is unacceptable if corrections to the record are required (either by the billing department, so it can issue a proper invoice to the customer, or by the customer service department in response to a customer complaint), or it is not delivered to billing by its nominal due date.

Figure 23.1 presents a time series plot featuring current performance and such a target. Since targets here are based on current performance, it may be appropriate or necessary to repeat baseline measurements. In Figure 23.1, the baseline is completed in three measurement intervals. Important components include the following:

- Immediate progress. Progress is demanded within six months. This will cause those charged with improvement to look for easy opportunities first.

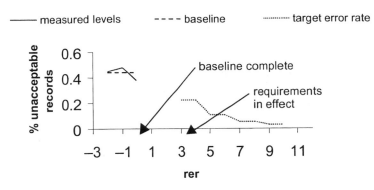

Figure 23.1   *Targets for improvement are based on a baseline*

- Long-term, dramatic progress. Continued progress in time and, in total, at least an order of magnitude improvement. Experience confirms
  that one to two orders of magnitude improvement are almost always
  attainable. Further, they "change the playing field," allow organizations to show definitive benefits, and build support for further improvements.

- Clear and aggressive time frames. In the first example, progress is
  demanded every six months. A bit of art is involved in setting time
  frames. Technically, the proper time frame should be linked to the
  rate of new data creation. If new data are created every month (as in
  many billing processes), halving the error rate in six months is reasonable. If new data are created daily, a shorter time frame is appropriate.

- Focus on the rate of improvement, rather than actual quality levels.
  People tend to react emotionally to measured quality levels. Those
  whose performance is poorer than they expect become defensive;
  those whose performance is better think they can rest on their laurels.
  But the data source that is improving the fastest will soon produce the
  best results, no matter how good its performance when it starts.

- Clear linkage to the business purpose. As discussed previously, the
  goal of reducing the billing department's workload is evident.

- Clear definition of the word "unacceptable."

- The focus on new data. Targets to complete a clean-up activity by
  such and such a date should be replaced with proactive goals such as:

  *Reduce the non–value-added work associated with data clean-up by half
  every six months, forever.*

- Another simple target may be based on the number of improvement projects completed every period of time. So a target to complete three improvement projects per quarter may also be a good target.

Field Tip 23.1: Demand aggressive rates of improvement.

24

Quality Planning—Designing New Information Chains

This chapter considers the question, "What if the data the customer requires don't exist. How are they to be obtained?"

The best data sources must innovate to create new data that answer new, as yet not clearly posed questions. This is how value is created in the new economy. Herein, we reserve the term "innovation" for something wholly new. We use the term "improvements" for changes to existing information chains. We recognize that sometimes one must innovate to improve.

This book emphasizes that good customers develop new data needs all the time. No sooner have they figured out how to integrate a new set of data into routine operations than they raise a whole host of new questions.

As a practical matter, no one source can meet the data needs of the entire organization. So a related question is, "How can one ensure high-quality data when they (the data) come from different sources?"

The answer to the first question can become quite involved, depending on the extent of new needs. But, generally, the situation is similar to that depicted in Figure 24.1. At least some portion of the new need may be met through an existing data source or sources, even though substantial improvements may be required. For data needs that cannot be met with existing sources, it is often the case that both a new data model (recall that models define what data mean) and a new information chain (for the actual data values) are required. Finally, it may happen that new functionality is required of information technology (IT).

The required steps are summarized in Figure 24.2. In effect, these steps involve nothing more than deploying each data quality requirement to the appropriate sources and ensuring that each source delivers. Existing information chains that don't meet requirements must be improved. Existing data models must be expanded or new ones developed via the organization's process for doing so. We have tacitly assumed that the organization has a

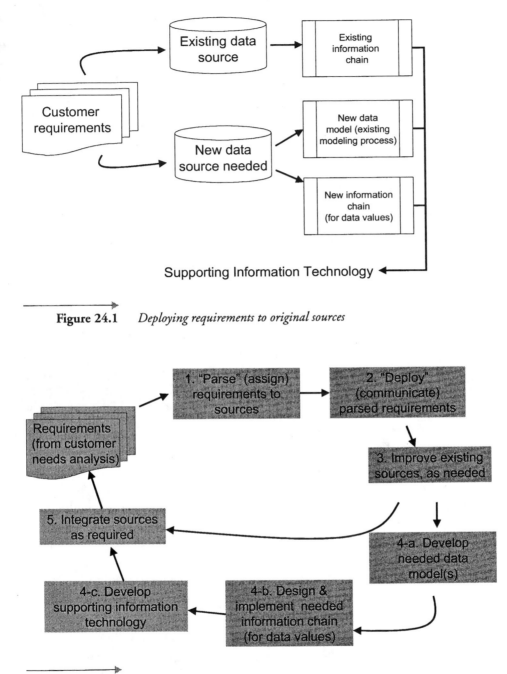

Figure 24.1   *Deploying requirements to original sources*

Figure 24.2   *Quality planning chain*

well-defined modeling chain for developing or otherwise obtaining new data models. This assumption may not be true, in which case it must be designed and implemented just like any other needed information chain. And new information chains must be designed (and then improved) to meet the requirements they have been assigned for ongoing creation of data values. Finally, supporting IT may be developed to automate the new information chain(s). We do wish to emphasize that the design of the information chain must proceed ahead of the supporting technology.

While the "science of new information chain design" is not very advanced, a number of principles have emerged and are listed in Table 24.1.

Table 24.1   *Principles of Information Chain Design*

Overall focus:

- ▓ Customer focus: Be very clear about the most important customers and their needs.
- ▓ Information chain owner and other roles, responsibilities: Remember that the information chain owner and those who will do the work are customers of the design/redesign. Design jobs people will like. Build in the tools that the information chain owner will need.
- ▓ Automation: Automate working processes. Do not automate a process that doesn't work in hope of a miracle. Miracles do occur, but counting on one is bad design practice.

Design principles:

- ▓ End-to-end focus: Optimize the end-to-end process, not subprocesses.
- ▓ Breadth: Bring in suppliers and customers when practical.
- ▓ Triage: Separate the simple from the "complex." Design the information chain to complete the simple quickly and well. Have specialists work the complex. In time, make the complex simple.
- ▓ Caseworkers (for information chains that require hand-offs between various departments): Employ caseworkers who are assigned to move work items along and ensure that none are lost in the cracks.
- ▓ JIT: Develop information products just-in-time to create needed value-added. This implies a pull, rather than push strategy. It also implies creating new data as late as possible (minimizing the need for changes due to normal churn).
- ▓ "Kitting": Use information kits, including raw data and instructions, at each step.
- ▓ Workflow tools: Use them to track progress and distribute kits.
- ▓ Data capture: Capture data as close to original sources as possible. People and subprocesses closest to the original data source are usually best.
- ▓ Cycle time reduction: Concentrate on eliminating queue time first.
- ▓ Eliminate duplication, bureaucracy, and steps that add no value.
- ▓ Minimize data transcription, data transformation, and redundant data storage.

Table 24.1   *Principles of Information Chain Design (continued)*

Design needed measurements into the new information chain:

- End-to-end measurement and control: Start with end-to-end measures that reflect the most critical customer needs. Include a control loop.
- Measurement of subprocesses: Most errors occur when work crosses organizational boundaries (i.e., the interfaces between subprocesses), so measure them.
- Suppliers: Include measurement of suppliers (if they don't measure themselves).
- Continuous improvement: Assume that the new information chain will not work perfectly and that it will experience continual changes. Build in the measurement capability to identify and eliminate root causes.

Design for error handling:

- Error proofing: Make it difficult to make errors (more easily said than done—people are very creative!).
- Exception processing: All work items that fall outside the process description (or are new to the specialists) should be clearly documented.
- Error correction: Make errors visible, easy to correct, and the source of opportunities for improvement.
- Data editing/clean-up: Apply data editing at data capture. Eschew designs that lead to periodic data clean-up.

Data design:

- Simple codes: Employ codes that are easily interpreted by almost everyone.
- Data dictionaries: Employ extensive data dictionaries and make them very easy to find and use. In particular, every account attribute should be clearly defined.

The steps shown in Figure 24.2 work equally when the targets are not information chains, but steps thereof. Rather than deploying requirements to separate sources, they (the requirements) are assigned to the pertinent step(s) within the information chain.

Field Tip 24.1: Several original data sources may be required to meet a customer's need. Deploy appropriate requirements to each source.

Field Tip 24.2: Emphasize communication of requirements to those expected to meet them.

Field Tip 24.3: Design new information chains to facilitate continuous improvement.

Field Tip 24.4: Design information chains first, then supporting information technology.

25

A Note on Reengineering

Reengineering is an important management tool that has enabled order-of-magnitude improvements in process performance—either speed, quality, or customer satisfaction.[1] The technique enjoyed a heyday in the late 1980s and early 1990s at a time when many large corporations needed to cut costs. Reengineering has gone out of favor due to several factors, including the following:

- Many people misunderstood where it should be applied. Corporations talked of "reengineering the IT department," whereas the technique was aimed at information chains.

- Many organizations failed to realize how hard reengineering was and did not have adequate change management.

- Reengineering projects had a high failure rate.

- Successful reengineering came to be associated with downsizing.

These points notwithstanding, reengineering is an important technique, though one to be used only when the situation demands. This chapter summarizes important points that those pursuing data quality must understand about reengineering and the top-line points the reengineer must understand about data quality.

First, the data quality perspective: The project-by-project approach to data quality improvement described in Chapter 22 is both incremental and "within the box." By "incremental," we mean that it produces slow but steady improvements. Slow but steady does not mean small. Over time, the accumulated impact can be substantial, and one to two orders of magnitude improvement are possible. By "within the box," we mean that it doesn't

---

1.   Consult Hammer or Davenport for descriptions.

force, or even necessarily encourage, people to think about customer needs and the information chain in new ways.

However there are situations when reengineering should be considered. These situations can include the following:

- The gap between customer needs and current performance is too large (and growing).

- A competitor has achieved a significant advantage (lower cost structure, meets customer needs better, etc.) through a better information chain.

- It is clear that thinking differently is required.

- One already has an idea that can, if successfully implemented, produce enormous advantages.

Also, if one or more of the following situations occur, consider reengineering:

- An organization can't routinely deliver a (correct) printed invoice and credit the proper customer.

- A competitor is using the Internet to invoice and receive payment and has a tremendous cost advantage.

- Customers are fleeing to your competitor in droves.

Viewed in that light, reengineering is basically an extension to quality improvement methodology.[2] Reengineering requires tremendous time (three years seems to be the minimum) and effort, and the risk of failure is high. A large organization can simultaneously conduct dozens, maybe even hundreds, of quality improvement projects. But one or two reengineering projects is the limit.

So an organization should use reengineering sparingly and only when there is no other choice and the payoff is worth it.

These warnings aside, there are several interesting relationships between data quality and reengineering. First, both reengineering and data quality cause the organization to think and act differently. Some of the social barriers are similar. And for both, it is important to actively manage change.

In this light, several descriptions in this book have pointed to the embedded "inspect and rework" loops within information chains (see, for

---

2.   While positioning reengineering this way is certainly logical and useful in some ways, it also seems incomplete. Unfortunately that view is simplistic.

example, Figure 3.1). Modifying the information chain to eliminate these non–value-added loops can be viewed as reengineering on a small scale.

The flip side is that the reengineered information chain should always be designed to eliminate these loops. Reengineering aims to get the "right (and correct) data in the right place at the right time to serve a customer," which is exactly the point of data quality as well. The principles of good design for data quality listed as Table 24.1 apply to reengineering as well.

Second, poor data quality can stymie reengineering. At the very least a reengineer should review the data quality requirements of the redesigned process (those who will do the work) and those impacted.

Third, and especially important, is that, once implemented, the reengineered information chain must be managed. It is best to name the information chain owner early and let him or her function as a customer for the redesign team.

Field Tip 25.1: At its heart, reengineering is about data. So reengineering teams should apply principles of good data quality design from the start.

Middle Management Roles and Responsibilities

There are two sources of new data: external suppliers and internal information chains. Supplier and information chain management (see Figure F.1) are the management techniques of choice to systematically apply the techniques described in Section E to data acquired from outside suppliers and data created internally, respectively. They are principle subjects of this section. Each is also a component of the ten common to most successful second-generation data quality systems (Chapter 15).

A number of common information chains (billing, data modeling, etc.) have been described throughout this book. Chapter 27 is directly relevant to these and other operational chains. Decision-making chains are a bit more involved. Guidelines for managing them are discussed in Chapter 28.

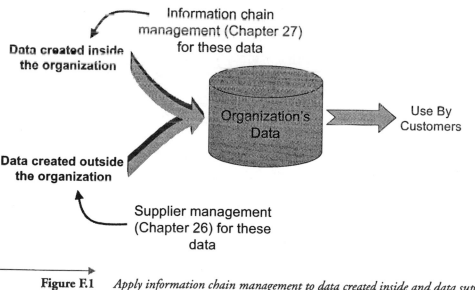

Figure F.1 *Apply information chain management to data created inside and data supplier management to data created outside the organization*

Finally, software tools to assist the data quality program are discussed in Chapter 29.

Field Tip F.1: Data are either created inside the organization or obtained from outside. Apply supplier management to data obtained from outside and apply information chain management to data created inside.

26

Data Supplier Management

Organizations acquire stunning amounts of data from outside sources. Much is bundled in some way with other products and services. Invoices received for these services are one example, manuals that describe how to use those products and services are another. Increasingly, of course, data are also purchased. Credit reports, market demographics, and financial reports are three common examples.

Clearly the organization requires these data to be of high quality. Indeed, most organizations want to simply put these data to use in operations and decision making. But before doing so, most organizations must check the quality of received data and make any needed corrections. It is a particularly virulent form of error detection and correction because it just becomes part of ongoing operations (option 3 in Chapter 10). It costs a lot of money and time and the supplier's underlying information chains do not get better. But organizations defend their actions, saying, "If those guys can't get us proper data, then we'll just have to do it ourselves."

A certain amount of error detection and correction may be needed in the short-term but, as rule 4 (Chapter 13) articulates, any form of clean-up without prevention is wrong-headed.

The prevention approach yields far better results. The structured method for doing so is called "data supplier management" and it effectively moves responsibility for quality back to the supplier. In doing so, it integrates the five techniques discussed previously (customer needs analysis, measurement, quality control, quality improvement, and planning) into a step-by-step procedure. In addition, data supplier management helps an organization identify its most important suppliers. Finally, supplier management enables an organization to simultaneously strengthen its suppliers and reduce its supplier base.

The most difficult aspect of supplier management for most organizations is coming to the realization that they have contributed to the inadequate data quality they currently receive. They believe that their suppliers are simply incompetent, don't care, don't have enough good people, or use old technology. Under direct examination, these explanations do not hold up. Rather, subtly, the organization has assumed responsibility for quality. It has done so through day-in and day-out actions to correct faulty data. It has not built the requirements and feedback channels that the customer-supplier model requires.

The situation may be likened to a young boy (a student), his homework, and his father's checking of that homework. The story begins innocently enough. The boy gets his first homework assignments, which he dutifully works on after dinner. His father, being the concerned parent and wishing him every success, checks his work. If the son answers any of the assigned problems incorrectly, his father patiently explains his son's mistake and the proper answer. All is well. The child gets a gold star on his homework and both parent and child feel good. And this pattern continues.

Unfortunately, as time goes on, the boy seems to miss more and more problems. By the last term of school, all the hard problems don't seem to be done very well. Of course the homework has gotten harder, but the effort doesn't seem to be there either. What has happened, subtly and slowly, is

Figure 26.1   *Cultural issue: It is easy for accountability to shift!*

that responsibility for the homework has shifted from the child to the parent (see Figure 26.1 for an illustration of this situation).

Importantly, neither the father nor the child did anything wrong. Both behaved normally. Most would agree the child is just doing what children do and the father is just being a good father. But their actions have led to a situation that neither the father desires nor is good for the boy. Finally, it is evident that if the situation is to change, the father must figure out how to shift responsibility for homework back to the boy. This is not to say that he cannot be involved in his son's homework. Indeed he must be. He just can't take responsibility for it.

Five styles of supplier management are presented in Figure 26.2. With the exception of rewards and penalties, they represent steps along a continuum from *caveat emptor* (buyer beware) to full partnerships. In a fully mature supplier management program, we note the following:

- There are a relatively few full partnerships reserved for those suppliers essential to the organization's long-term survival or success.

Approach	Major Features	
1. Status Quo	Continue on current path	First generation
2. Quality Baselining/Ongoing Reporting	Customer: Define and communicate DQ requirements. Supplier: Baseline performance against requirements. Supplier: Remeasure at regular intervals.	First generation
3. Proactive Customer-Supplier Relationship	Customer: Define and communicate DQ requirements. Supplier: Baseline performance against requirements. Jointly: Agree on targets for improvement. Supplier: Pursue improvements. Remeasure at regular intervals.	Second generation
4. Rewards/Penalties	"Targets" above become performance standards. Compare ongoing measurements against standards. Apply rewards or penalties.	Second generation
5. Partnership	Objective: Long-term relationship with an excellent supplier. Requirements and measurements from above. Both customer and supplier invest (time) to ensure that gaps are closed expeditiously.	Second generation

Figure 26.2   *Approaches to data supplier management*

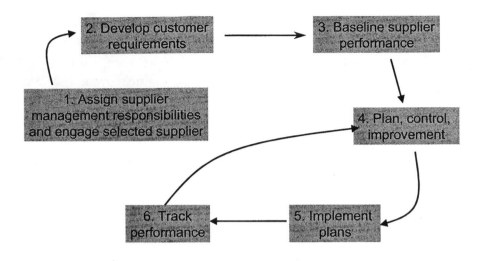

Figure 26.3   *Data supplier management cycle*

- Most relationships fall into the proactive customer-supplier management category.

- A few relationships, with new data suppliers (or new data and information products) are not as far along.

- The organization has fewer suppliers.

The supplier management cycle is summarized in Figure 26.3. It is the basis for advancing and maintaining a proactive customer-supplier relationship. Note that the cycle itself consists of five steps, and there are two steps outside the cycle. As noted previously, the cycle represents a structured way of integrating the technical methods discussed in this book. Specifically, step 2 involves customer needs, step 3 measurement, and steps 4–6 planning, control, and improvement. Importantly, step 1 calls for assigning a supplier manager to coordinate the program with each supplier. As with all data quality roles and responsibilities, this one should be clearly assigned.

Few organizations, given their current patterns of thinking, jump into supplier management all at once. Instead they begin with one or two prototypes. So step 0 involves selecting those first suppliers. Many organizations agonize over this issue, but it need not be that difficult. There are no hard and fast rules for doing so, beyond balancing the following considerations:

- Importance to the business

- Known issues with supplier data

- Supplier willingness to experiment together for several months (high-level connections can often secure this willingness—but early on, if a supplier doesn't want to participate, find another that does)

- Ease of meeting face to face

Organizations with hundreds (thousands) of data suppliers may be unable to invest the time that proactive customer-supplier management requires with all suppliers. Such organizations should divide their suppliers into three categories, as follows:

1. The critical suppliers, for whom it must effect proactive supplier management

2. The important suppliers, for whom a form of supplier certification is in order—the certification aims to ensure that the supplier properly uses the methods of this *Field Guide*.

3. The unimportant suppliers—those the organization could just as well do without

Key elements of a certification program are depicted in Figure 26.4. Earning certification requires rigorous effort by suppliers. At a minimum they must understand customer needs, make and share good measurements, effect control and continuous improvement, and have a management structure that leads and supports these activities.

To conclude this chapter, we note that the biggest obstacles to data supplier management are political and social. This despite the enormous success of supplier management in manufacturing and current interest in electronic bonding and supply chain management. Supplier management, as described here, changes entrenched ways of doing things. (Chapters 33–34 consider social and political issues more completely.) Two common concerns are:

1. "We can't force a particular supplier to participate. And they're awful!"

2. "How will we protect ourselves? We just can't trust them."

The best way to address the first concern is simple: Don't force a supplier to participate. Instead, help the supplier understand what it will gain and let it make its own decision. Early on, it has the opportunity to learn more about how customers use its data. Or it may be able to improve customer satisfaction and gain a measure of advantage. Avoid motherhood-and-apple-

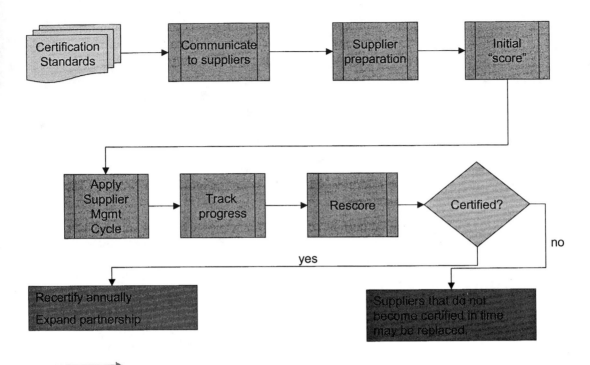

Figure 26.4   *Supplier certification process*

pie reasons such as, "It is in their enlightened self-interest to do so." Figure out tangible benefits that motivate the supplier.

Later, the supplier may decide to participate from fear of being left out. If a supplier adamantly refuses to improve over the long haul, a new supplier must be found. This may be difficult, but the alternative is even worse.

The second concern involves trusting the vendor and protecting the organization. The supplier management cycle addresses these concerns by requiring measurement by the supplier. The customer organization knows the quality of supplied data (good, bad, or indifferent), because quality levels are measured and reported. And the measurement process may be audited. Trust is built slowly in time, as measured results indicate improvements.

Protection leads many companies to require rewards and penalties in their contracts (suppliers will be induced to provide high quality because they get more money and we'll be protected if they don't). In principle, rewards and penalties sound like a good idea. But they are difficult to administer. They often lead to contention between customer and supplier.

They do not help build partnerships. Rewards and penalties may occasionally be appropriate, but use them sparingly and with great care.

Field Tip 26.1: A good area to start the data quality program is with critical data suppliers.

Field Tip 26.2: Most data suppliers want to provide high-quality data and are in dire need of good requirements. The leaders, those who first articulate clear requirements and keep them current, are almost always heard.

Field Tip 26.3: Data supplier managers should be named and held accountable for advancing the supplier management cycle.

Field Tip 26.4: "Partnership" may be the most over-used word in business lingo. Reserve it for those few suppliers on whom you absolutely depend.

Field Tip 26.5: Within the organization, it is often appropriate to apply supplier management to the other departments on which one depends.

27

Managing Information Chains

We now turn our attention to the flow of data created internally. Even casual observation confirms that most data flow horizontally, from department to department, rather than vertically, through the chain of command. Data created by the order entry department wind their way to shipping, then to billing and accounts receivable, then to finance, and so forth. Along the way new data and information products are created. Order entry creates a customer order sheet, shipping creates a bill of lading (that external customers may receive), billing creates an invoice, and so forth.

While each department could manage upstream departments as data suppliers using the supplier management cycle, there is a better way. The most critical information chains should be explicitly managed horizontally or cross-functionally.

The information chain management cycle is the preferred technique for managing critical information chains. A process is any sequence of work activities, characterized by common inputs and outputs and directed to a common goal. An "information chain" is a category of process in which the inputs and outputs are data and information.

Figure 27.1 illustrates the sequence of steps. There are many similarities between the information chain and data supplier management cycles: the assignment of management responsibilities, customer needs, measurement, control, and improvement. The biggest exception involves "describe the information chain." While it may be desirable to flowchart a supplier's information chains, *how* a supplier does its work is usually not of interest.

Even mediocre implementation of information chain management yields stunning improvements in data quality (just as supplier management does). One important reason is that it focuses attention on a weakness in most organizations: the white space of the organizational chart. Actually, most departments in most organizations are really pretty good. To the

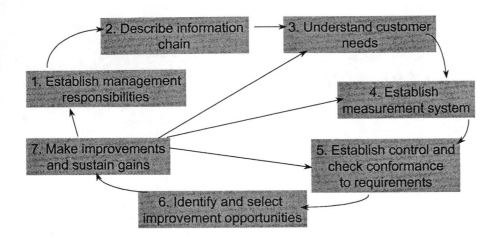

Figure 27.1   *Information chain management cycle*

degree that departments and people within them understand their roles, they complete them rather well. They actually enter orders, ship products, and invoice pretty well.

But most departments don't talk to each other very much. So needed communications channels, as called for in the customer-supplier model, are ad hoc at best.

The lack of communication is especially damaging to data quality because, as noted previously, data move horizontally between departments. Information chain management facilitates effective communication. And departments, once they understand what is required downstream, are usually able to adjust their activities to make needed improvements.

Further, the sequence of work activities along many, perhaps even most, information chains is similar to that depicted in Figure 24.2. Each department's work consists of a long queue, finding and correcting any errors in data received from upstream (a virulent form of option 3, Chapter 10, in which data quality efforts are embedded in day-in-and day-out work. This is another example of responsibility for data quality shifting, subtly or otherwise, downstream from its creation), completing its value-added work, and setting its completed work in the next department's queue. At least half of the activities are non-value-added. They increase the cycle time (the end-to-end time needed to complete one instance of the information chain). And the numerous hand-offs increase the chances for error.

There are any number of ways to improve upon information chains similar to that shown in Figure 24.2. All involve some combination of:

- Eliminating, or at least minimizing, inspection and rework of data. Advance the data quality system to do so. Either upstream activities become part of the information chain or are managed via supplier management.

- Minimizing queue time to speed things up. Interestingly, when people hear that "We must speed up the process," their immediate reaction is that they must work harder or faster (or maybe that they need faster computers). Naturally they don't like this. But it is almost always the case that most of the end-to-end cycle time is eaten up in queues. Better designs (see Chapter 24) to minimize queues are far more effective.

- Minimizing handoffs through cross-functional work teams, and so on.

Information chain management is stunningly effective. It can improve information chains in the following ways:

- Reduce error rates by one to two orders of magnitude

- Cut the time required for a unit of work to flow through the end-to-end information chain by factors of two to ten

- Reduce the cost of poor data quality by up to two-thirds

Yet information chain management is very threatening, especially to middle managers. Many fear that their jobs will be eliminated and the evidence seems to bear out their fears. Millions of jobs have been lost through downsizing as companies reengineered their processes. And if the non–value-added work shown in Figure 27.2 is eliminated, there will be less work to manage, hence fewer middle managers will be required. While there is no hard evidence to back it up, this *Field Guide* strongly suspects that managers interested in accumulating power, as measured by the size of their departments or budgets, are especially threatened by information chain management. At the very least, information chain management upsets existing reporting relationships, and middle managers find their roles change dramatically.

Unfortunately, there is no silver bullet to help address these concerns. Enlightened organizations may try to reduce them by promising that jobs

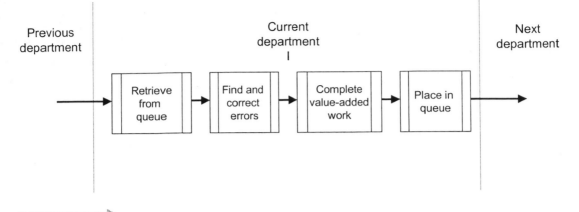

Figure 27.2 *A typical information chain crosses many departments*

will not be lost due to quality efforts, but few employees really believe it. The simple advice to the organization is as follows:

- Do not be surprised that people are threatened.

- At least initially, don't replace the organizational chart with an information chain structure. Overlay the management teams for the most important information chains on the existing structure (see Chapter 32).

- Senior leadership is essential for successful implementation.

- It may be best to gain some experience with supplier management first (Chapter 26).

- Actively manage change (Chapter 33).

Field Tip 27.1: Recognize that data flow horizontally across the organization. The most important such "flows" should be explicitly managed as information chains.

Field Tip 27.2: Recognize that a department's efforts to find and correct data received from upstream is non–value-added work and adds time and expense. For the most important information chains, information chain management is the technique of choice for minimizing this non-value-added work.

Field Tip 27.3: In most cases, it will be middle managers who most tenaciously resist information chain management because it most impacts their jobs.

Field Tip 27.4: To start, identify a few critical information chains and form a (senior) cross-functional team to manage the chain end to end.

28

Making Better Decisions

Decision makers and planners are highly dependent on data. They almost always depend on facts on which to base their decisions.[1] Except by dumb luck, decisions can be no better than the data on which they are based. And, quite naturally, managers are concerned that wrong decisions will impact their careers. So most managers, at the very least, want to be able to defend their decisions with data. In building the case for a data quality program (Chapters 7–9) we noted that the potential impact of poor data on one's career may strike more closely to home than the impact on the organization. The fact that "We're losing millions due to poor billing" just doesn't have the cachet of "I'll be blamed if this decision is wrong."

This chapter is concerned with decision chains, a type of information chain that produces answers to questions of a tactical nature. The terms "strategic," "tactical," and "operational" have not and will not be defined, except in relation to one another. For most people, "strategy" is what people two levels above them do, their role is "tactics," and "operations" is what people two levels below them do. These working definitions are adequate for the purposes of this chapter. Some typical questions are as follows:

- What promotion should we launch to increase market share in sector B-11 by 2 percent?

- Is it likely that we will meet our budget commitments?

- Are customers seeing the results of improvements made to the ignition system?

- Are our efforts to reduce cycle time working?

Another name for decision chains is "measurement chains." Some people prefer that term because it emphasizes what they believe to be the most

---

1. There are, of course, plenty of exceptions. Many managers have operated from the seats of their pants their entire careers and don't want to be confused by the facts.

difficult step—making relevant, accurate, and timely measurements of customer satisfaction, market share, cycle time, or whatever. (This author disagrees. I believe that the most difficult step is implementing the decision. See the following text.)

Different managers, instinctively perhaps, use different criteria in making their decisions. Some are more risk averse than others. Some are more long-term oriented than others. Some are concerned with standing out, others with blending in. Thus, an important step in managing a decision chain involves framing the problem/opportunity to be addressed and the overall context in which decisions are made.

Decisions are rarely made on the basis of a single fact. Rather, managers accumulate facts and organize them in different ways. They try to fill gaps in their facts by seeking more or new data. And they may consider the extent to which the facts support various options.

Importantly, the point of view taken in this *Field Guide* is that a decision chain does not end with a manager's decision. Implementation is all important. While the claim is not scientifically defensible, most organizations are far worse at aligning departments and people to take the appropriate actions than they are at actually making decisions.

This observation reinforces the point that a decision chain ends not with the decision, but rather with the actions taken. It seems as though the most important impact of poor data quality on decision making is not that suboptimal decisions result, but rather that decisions take too long to make, are not made with confidence, and can't be implemented properly. This also explains why important decisions are rarely made by a single individual. Rather, they are made, or at least ratified, by a group. And, ideally at least, the group consists of those who must implement the decision.

A working model of a generic decision chain is presented as Figure 28.1. The figure is simplistic in that it describes a highly iterative series of steps as linear. That criticism aside, the figure illustrates what must be done.

The figure also illustrates how effective decision chains apply the techniques of data quality management described throughout this book, particularly the following:

- The end-to-end decision chain is managed like any other information chain. This point is counterintuitive to many managers. They feel that the circumstances surrounding each and every decision are unique. So there is no common decision chain. While this *Field Guide* does not dispute that occasionally circumstances are unique, most are not. Human resources is well advised to manage "candidate

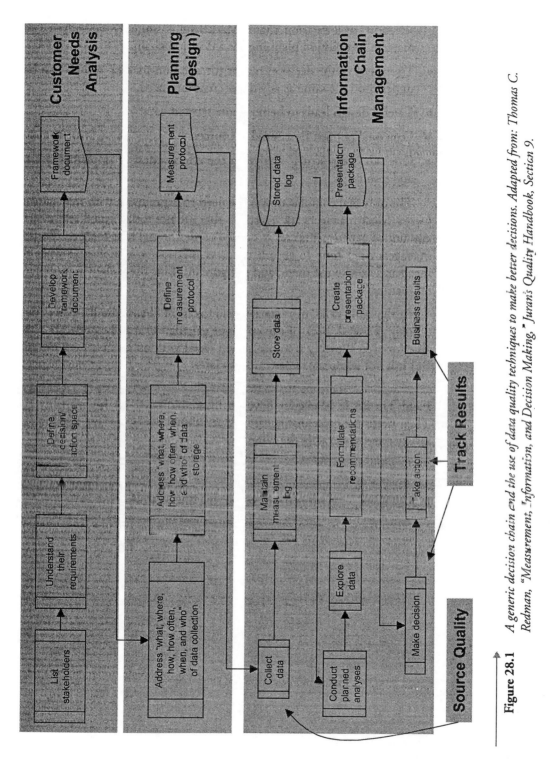

Figure 28.1 *A generic decision chain and the use of data quality techniques to make better decisions. Adapted from: Thomas C. Redman, "Measurement, Information, and Decision Making," Juran's Quality Handbook, Section 9.*

selection" as a decision chain. Marketing is similarly well-advised to manage "promotion planning" as a decision chain.

- The needs of the decision maker (or decision-making group) can be understood the same as any other customer need.

- Careful design leads to better, more trusted data.

- Data quality must be assured at sources.

- One can "keep score," analyzing the effectiveness of implementation and results.

The only real complication is the need to experiment with new measurements. Most managers ask questions that are not well formed and a certain amount of experimentation is needed to define the best metrics. Similarly, managers need time to absorb the new metrics, to understand what they mean and how to use them, and to figure out how they relate to more familiar metrics.

At the same time, new metrics and decision chains should evolve rather quickly. A useful, back-of-the-envelope calculation may be perfectly acceptable (or even the only recourse) when faced with an entirely new situation. But it is not acceptable a few months later.

Field Tip 28.1: Managers have an insatiable need for high-quality data. Their needs are quite distinct from operational needs, but the techniques to satisfy them are exactly the same.

Field Tip 28.2: Manage decision making like any other information chain.

29

Tools

There are dozens of good tools on the market to assist the organization in its data quality efforts. (A friend once remarked that he thought the most important technological advance in data quality had been 3-M's Post-It Note.) However, only the following three tools are essential:

1. A good measurement tool to quantify data quality levels

2. A good, basic statistical package to construct control charts and Pareto charts and support root cause analysis

3. A basic project management tool to keep track of the status of various projects

Other tools become increasingly useful as the data quality program matures. These include the following:

- Scorecard tools (executive information systems) to support summary presentation of results to the data council (Chapter 30)

- Workflow tools to assist information chain owners

- In-line editors to signal simple input errors such as data are being created

- Data repositories to automate the storage and management of data resource data

And, of course, sooner or later, many organizations require a data clean-up tool (hopefully to bring the data within a database up to the quality standards of newly created data). Finally, there are more advanced tools such as simulators (to experiment with process improvements). These are beyond the scope of this book.

Measurement tools aim to quantify data quality levels. While initial measurements of error rates can be made by hand, this eventually becomes tedious and a measurement tool is needed. Essentially, measurement tools do no more than automate the spreadsheet presented in Figure 18.2. They spot data values that fail business rules and make the appropriate counts. As such, they may use the same error detection engines as clean-up tools, many of which ignore the needed counts. Error detection engines can be quite sophisticated. Especially early on, there is usually no need to detect sophisticated errors, since the focus is on eliminating the root causes of the more numerous simple errors. A simple user interface and nice graphical summaries are the most important features to look for.

Second most important is a statistical tool to draw control charts, make Pareto charts, and support further root cause analysis. The most important features are a simple user interface, outstanding graphical summaries, and excellent data management capabilities. Sophisticated analyses are not required.

Third is a project management tool. All quality work is horribly detailed (and the vultures are quick to gather when a data quality guy makes a simple mistake). So a decent project management tool is needed when the number of projects increases beyond the number that can be easily tracked by hand.

Many organizations today are implementing balanced scorecards to integrate the most important summary measurements of performance from various perspectives—financial, customer, internal business process, and so forth. A similar data quality scorecard, integrating results of the most important suppliers and information chains, is useful for data councils and supplier management alike. In time, summary data quality measures may become part of balanced scorecards. Supporting technologies are sometimes called executive information systems, and many good ones are available.

Workflow tools help automate information chains. Most employ a simple drawing tool, which allows the information chain owner to describe the flow of work and data, from input to creation of new data and information products. Relatively simple pictures highlight value-added and non-value-added work and the departmental interfaces needed to complete work. Workflow may also include simulation tools, which allow the information chain owner to experiment with new designs. Finally, workflow tools can automate the hand-off of individual work items as they wind their way through the information chain.

In-line editors are checkers that validate data entry. They effect controls to prevent errors from leaking through (Chapter 20). Thus, when a clerk enters a customer's address, an in-line editor will validate that it (the entered address) really is a valid address and, if not, suggest possible corrections. The editing procedure involves determining if data values satisfy business rules. For addresses in the United States, these rules are given in the Postal Standard and are available from the United States Postal Service. Software tools implement the standard. Good ones also suggest corrections. For example, the address "34 Sycamore Avenue, Little Silver, NJ 07730, cannot be correct. The best tools recognize that "34 Sycamore Avenue, Little Silver, NJ" is valid and suggest 07739 as the zip code.

In-line editors are applied within an information chain, so data that are identified as flawed are not passed downstream. Used properly in conjunction with a measurement tool, in-line editors are an effective means to improve and control data entry. But they can be misused. Data entry personnel soon learn how to bypass the editor. The result is a false sense of security that data values "passed QC and so must be of high quality." Finally, editors require continual maintenance as business rules change.

Data repositories are specially designed databases for data resource data. There are many good repositories available to serve the needs of developers. But the most important feature is a simple interface through which the data customer can find answers to basic questions about the meaning of data.

The market for clean-up tools is richly developed and many good ones are available. As discussed in Chapters 10–13, data clean-up must only be employed when the situation is dire. Despite the good tools, data clean-up is difficult and time consuming. Finding lots of errors is relatively easy, finding all of them and making corrections requires skilled human intervention. Thus, clean-up tools, are actually misnamed. A better name would be "error identification tools," because that is what most actually do.

As for using clean-up tools, the biggest issues are developing the business rules and ensuring that the tool scales to the size of the clean-up effort. Some clean-up tools are of the general-purpose variety, allowing the user to define his or her domains of allowed data values. Others, such as those based on the Postal Standard, come fully equipped with rules. The advantages of each are readily apparent.

Scalability is a bit trickier and beyond the scope of this book. Fortunately, most IT departments are well aware of scalability issues and can provide needed support.

A final word regarding data quality tools. Quite naturally, their makers extol their virtues on the basis of technical superiority, general applicability, and an approach built around their tool. This book recommends that information chains be designed first, then supported by technology. For example, an information chain owner should first decide how he or she wishes to make the measurements, then select a tool to do so, rather than the other way around.

Field Tip 29.1: It is almost always better to pick specific tools to solve specific problems than to pick general tools to solve general problems.

Why Senior Management Must Lead and What It Must Do

The subject of this section is the things senior management must contribute to the data quality program. In terms of our model of successful second-generation data quality systems (Chapter 15), senior management provides three elements: senior leadership and support, data policy, and managing the data culture.

Why is senior leadership needed? Left on their own, powerful forces deter middle managers from successfully implementing supplier and information chain management. Senior management must, at the very least, mitigate these forces. After all, poor data quality is not a phenomenon that has appeared from nowhere all of a sudden. Instead, poor data quality is largely the result of actions, some conscious, most not, taken over the years. For example, most management is done "up and down" the organization chart, while most data flows across it.

30

Senior Leadership and Support

Senior management must lead the data quality program if it is to be widely implemented. Middle managers, through skunk works and individual initiative, can get the program started. And most can effect the needed changes within their chains of command, but they simply do not have the influence needed for the data quality program to penetrate the entire organization. More than any other factors, the seniority and breadth of the individuals perceived to be leading the effort dictate the penetration of improved data quality (and hence the returns). The more senior the better. The broader the better.

Said differently, the best approaches to data quality require people to think and act differently (Chapter 34 discusses culture change). And achieving the one to two orders of magnitude improvement for all important data, suppliers, and information chains is demanding. The risks of failure decrease with broad, powerful senior leadership.

Data councils are one (but by no means the only) way of providing the necessary leadership. Alternatively, the council can be an existing committee, such as the operations committee. Ideally, a data council is chaired by the chief executive or operating officer or equivalent (some departments may also wish to implement data councils—they could be chaired by chief financial officers, marketing vice presidents, etc.).

Councils have the following responsibilities:

- Leading the data quality effort
- Deploying management responsibilities for data (Chapters 31 and 32)
- Supporting information chain and supplier management (Chapters 26 and 27)
- Managing the "data culture" (Chapters 33 and 34)

- Ensuring that data quality efforts are adequately funded. (Note that although improved data quality pays outstanding returns, the current costs are buried in other ongoing activities, so it may be necessary to provide "seed money.")

A more complete list of the specific items is provided in Table 30.1. It is evident from this table that leading the data quality effort is real work. Joseph Juran, explaining many of the early failures of quality management

Table 30.1   *Roles and Responsibilities of Senior Management*

I. **Lead the data quality program**

    A. Formulate business case

        1. Most important issues/opportunities relevant to data (i.e., cost reduction, customer satisfaction, competitive advantage, etc.)

        2. Expected returns

    B. Formulate and promulgate quality policy

        1. Role of data quality to organization's strategy

        2. Managerial responsibilities

        3. Targets for continuous improvement

        4. Contribution to merit rating

    C. Select major dimensions of data quality

        1. In customers' eyes (accuracy, timeliness, relevancy, etc.)

        2. With respect to the competition

        3. Cost of poor data quality (i.e., error detection and correction)

    D. Communication of all of the above to important stakeholders, including key customers, employees, etc.

II. **Support information chain and supplier management**

    A. Identify the most important processes and suppliers

    B. Invest information chain and supplier managers with the needed authority

    C. Establish the "project system," including machinery for

        1. soliciting project nominations

        2. selecting projects

        3. chartering project teams

        4. selecting the teams (leaders, members, facilitators, etc.)

        5. supporting project teams

        6. reviewing results

        7. celebrating success

        8. ensuring that improvements are sustained

Table 30.1 *Roles and Responsibilities of Senior Management (continued)*

III. Advancing the data culture

    A. Advancing the concept of data "as business assets"

    B. Leading change management efforts

    C. Motivating continuous improvement

    D. Resolving issues (such as those of "data ownership") as they occur

    E. Ensuring that the training program is in place

        1. Data curriculum

            a. Process and supplier management

            b. Planning, control, and improvement processes

            c. Problem solving, team building, group dynamics

        2. Style of training

IV. Ensuring adequate funding

A. For training

B. For data quality staff (see Chapter 32)

in manufacturing, remarked, "They thought they could make the right speeches, establish broad goals, and leave everything else to subordinates. . . . They didn't realize that fixing quality meant fixing whole companies, a task that can't be delegated."[1]

In some respects, it may be even more difficult to lead a quality program for data. After all, data are intangible, and bad data seem to strike like viruses (there is no telling where they'll turn up next). Further, it is so easy to confuse data or information with the supporting technology. And data seem to engender passion and politics like no other asset.

Field Tip 30.1: For maximum impact, senior management must lead data quality efforts. Senior managers who eschew their data responsibilities seem not to understand the importance of data and information in the Information Age.

1. Joseph M. Juran, "Made in USA: A Renaissance in Quality," *Harvard Business Review* (July–August 1993):47.

31

Crafting a Data Policy

If this *Field Guide* could offer only one prescription, it would be this:

> *Assign responsibility for the quality of data to those who create them. If this is not possible, assign responsibility as close to data creation as possible.*

If followed, this prescription offers excellent odds that future data errors will be prevented; that information chain and supplier managers will be effective; and that customer needs, measurement, control, improvement, and planning techniques will be consistently applied where needed most.

While there are plenty of exceptions, work that is not explicitly assigned is not pursued aggressively in most organizations. Data quality can be especially difficult. Though data are everywhere, they are also intangible and people tend not to think much about them. Absent clearly assigned responsibilities, data quality is left to individual initiative. Therefore, this *Field Guide* recommends that an explicit policy be developed and implemented by the data council to clarify proper roles.

It is evident that assigning responsibility for data quality to the quality department or the data department is insufficient. More to the point, many organizations assign responsibility for data quality to the chief information officer, the IT department, or equivalent. While IT may bear responsibility for some aspects of data quality (if, for example, it creates data models), it is important that "I" (data and information) not be confused with "IT" (information technology) (see Chapter 5). These departments simply do not create much data, so they cannot be held accountable for much. As a practical matter, these departments can do no more than clean up erred data, exactly what the organization wants to avoid.

Further, many people and departments touch data and hence may impact quality in some way. Some examples follow (refer to the dimensions of data quality presented in Chapter 17):

- Data modelers (or analysts) create data models and so may impact the relevancy (comprehensiveness, etc.) of data to the issue at hand.

- Database administrators and others create data resource data (metadata) or data libraries and so may impact a data customer's ability to find or understand data.

- Information chains provide new data values and so impact accuracy, timeliness, and other dimensions.

- Information technologists provide computer systems and other information technology and so may impact a data customer's ability to access data.

- Developers create and maintain applications programs through which data customers access and use data and so may impact their ability to interpret data.

- Database administrators maintain databases and as a result may impact security.

- Help desk staffers answer questions and so may impact the utility of data.

- Data architects provide data architectures that may impact how data are named and interrelate.

- Those who use data interpret them and so impact their appropriate use.

- External suppliers provide the whole package and so may impact almost all of the above.

Fortunately, it is relatively easy to apply the prescription given above and specify a policy that covers these examples. The left side of Figure 31.1 highlights the main points. The right side addresses other important issues, including the following:

- The specific roles of the data council (or its equivalent)

- The need for and roles of a support staff

- The related issues of data sharing and data ownership

Regarding the role of the data council, since management responsibility for data under this policy is so diffuse, strong leadership from the council is

Typical Management Accountabilities for Dimensions of Data Quality

Categories of Dimensions of Data Quality*	Typical Management Responsibility for Data Obtained from Outside the Organization	Typical Management Responsibility for Data Created within the Organization
Accessibility and Delivery	Relevant supplier and supplier manager	Information Technology Department
Data Models	Relevant supplier and supplier manager	Data Modeling Process Owner
Data Values	Relevant supplier and supplier manager	Information Chain Owners
Presentation Quality	Relevant supplier and supplier manager	Application Development Process Owner**
Improvement	Relevant supplier and supplier manager	Relevant Information Chain and Process Owners
Privacy	Relevant supplier and supplier manager	Data Customers
Commitment of Source	Relevant supplier and supplier manager	Relevant Information Chain and Process Owners
Architecture	Relevant supplier and supplier manager	Architecture Process Owners

*For a list of the dimensions in each category, see Table 17.1.
**In most cases, data customers gain access to data via an "application." If the application is purchased, the supplier is responsible for dimensions associated with data presentation.

Essential Elements of a Data Policy

Overall:

1. Data and information, the information chains that create, manipulate, and use data and information, and supporting information technologies are the property of the entire organization.
2. A department must share the data it creates or otherwise obtains, unless privacy, security or legal constraints dictate otherwise. A sharing organization may recover its costs of doing so.
3. Permission to share data outside the boundaries of the organization (such as via Web sites) must be obtained from the Data Council or its representative.

The data council bears overall responsibility for data quality. It must implement this policy, including policies for security, privacy, and data ownership and sharing. It must support supplier and information chain managers, advance the data culture, and provide needed funding. The council must provide for a Conflict Resolution Board to address issues as they arise. The council (or its staff) must provide a number of centralized functions, as follows:

- Communications
- Tools and training
- Project infrastructure
- "Standards," such as for common terms or best practice
- Overall summaries of progress and areas for improvement
- Assist with/lead especially difficult or important projects

All external suppliers of data are fully accountable for the data they provide. Suppliers must implement customer needs, measurement, and control, improvement and planning projects as needed. A supplier management function will help suppliers understand our needs, select priorities, and so forth. That function notwithstanding, suppliers are responsible for the data they supply.

Owners of information chains are fully accountable for the data (including the data models and data values their processes create). They must implement customer needs, measurement, and control, improvement and planning projects as needed.

The Information Technology Department must develop and implement technologies that make data safe and secure, easy to access and share, and keep unit cost reasonable.

Figure 31.1   *Essential elements of a data policy*

absolutely essential. For this reason, the roles and responsibilities of the council should explicitly be included as part of the policy.

Since the council must both be so senior and so active, it must usually have a small staff to carry out its day-in and day-out work. The staff can also acquire expertise in data quality and lead efforts that departments will not. For example, if standard definitions of key terms such as "customer" or "sale" are needed, the data council's staff can coordinate the development of such a standard. (See also Chapter 32 for a discussion about standards.)

Issues of data ownership and data sharing can be especially tough. On the one hand, it seems appealing to assign ownership to databases or important categories of data. At the very least, accountability is clear.[1] But owners have certain rights and privileges, such as the rights to withhold data and to sell them under the best terms they can get. The consequences can be enormous and include the following:

- Access to data owned by one department may be denied another.
- The owning department may set terms and conditions that another cannot meet.
- The denied department may seek to develop its own database. And the consequence is a wider gap between the two departments.
- The owning department may desire to sell the data outside the organization.

These issues can be very divisive and lead us to conclude that, as a matter of policy, most data cannot be owned. Managers and organizations have specific accountabilities and rights, but they cannot own data.

At the same time, data sharing is much more difficult than one might think. If knowledge is power in the Information Age, and people and organizations wish to acquire power, then they will not share data, or even let others become aware of their existence. First, the organization has legitimate security needs. Second, the receiving department is, in effect, a new customer, with slightly different needs. Third, there can be any number of technical issues, each seemingly trivial, that take time and cost money to resolve. A good data policy can provide some relief by outlining terms and conditions under which data sharing should occur.

1. Results are mixed. Many people/organizations that assign accountability for data to specific people or organizations achieve solid first-generation data quality systems, often a great improvement. But they cannot break through to second-generation systems, so improvements are limited.

Field Tip 31.1: The first principle of data quality management: Assign responsibility for the quality of data to those who create them. If this is not possible, assign responsibility as close to data creation as possible.

Field Tip 31.2: Data ownership is a slippery slope. On paper, the concept makes good sense, but it presents dangers. Managers and departments must have specific accountabilities and rights, but they cannot own data.

32

Organizing for Data Quality

The proposed organizational structure to promote data quality is presented in Figure 32.1. This structure is to be laid on top of the current organization, rather than replace it.

One might expect that organizational structures well tuned to the rigors of the Information Age would have emerged by now. Indeed, existing organizational structures have not, so far at least, been particularly accommodating to data. While there is considerable experimentation with self-managed work teams, flatter hierarchies, and so-called network organizations, the canonical organizational structure for the Information Age is not yet clear. Until this happens, overlaying organizational components to advance the data quality program seems the best choice.

The structure proposed in Figure 32.1, its limitations aside, does offer considerable advantages, including the following:

- It features three levels and makes the responsibilities of each level clear. At the top is a leadership and support level and at the bottom are the project teams completing customer needs, measurement, control, and planning projects. Middle management assumes responsibility for the major data sources, via management roles for information chains and suppliers.

- It recognizes critical roles played by cross-functional information chains. Information chain management teams may be composed of individuals across functions.

- It ensures that lower levels are supported from above. Those struggling with demanding projects may seek the aid of information chain and supplier managers, and information chain and supplier managers may look to the data council.

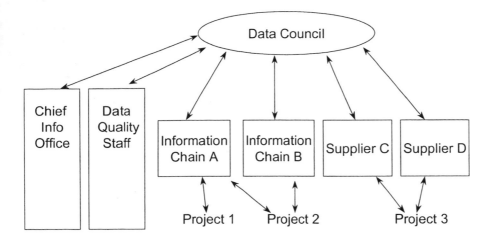

Figure 32.1   *Proposed organization for data quality (overlaid on current organization)*

- It provides the means for excellent communication. First, for vertical communication, senior management is only two levels removed from the details and so has a means to become informed of the real issues. Similarly, managers and people working on projects are close enough to leadership to understand the connections between data and business success. Information chain and supplier management provides horizontal communication.

- It clearly separates "I" (data and information) from "IT" (information technology). It ensures that data are not subordinated to information technology, as often happens when a chief information officer is assigned responsibility for data quality.

- It provides for a small staff (the responsibilities of which are described in Chapter 31).

- It causes a minimum of disruption to existing business relationships. The process structure is most difficult. While today (late 2000), most organizations recognize that most work gets accomplished through processes, they have not yet implemented a process-centric organization.

Field Tip 32.1: Managing data quality is hard enough without organizational mischief. So overlay the needed structures for leadership and support, information chain and supplier management, and all projects on the existing organizational chart.

33

Recognizing Social Issues

All data and data quality issues have social dimensions (it is just as accurate to call these "political dimensions," but to some the term "political" has negative implications). What is most amazing is that people still seem surprised by this. Comments such as "We'd really be able to do some impressive things if only the politics would go away," "You can't trust that supplier. They have a virtual monopoly," and "We'd be fine if only we could get a common definition of 'customer'" are the norm.

But contention for and about critical resources is not only normal, it is healthy. This is especially true with new resources[1] such as data.[2] Be aware of social issues and proactively address them as part of the data quality program. At least avoid issues that will harm it. This chapter describes a number of social issues and suggests steps to help resolve or mitigate them. Chapter 34 considers steps to address them more holistically.

Figures 33.1 through 33.8 present a series of graphics that depict common social issues. Five of these issues and, in some cases, steps to resolve them, have been discussed elsewhere in this book. The following list briefly summarizes these issues:

- *Issue: The ease with which responsibility for data quality slips downstream away from those who create the data* (Figure 33.1). For example, an organization takes responsibility for the quality of data it purchases by first scanning them to identify and correct any obvious errors. This issue can disguise itself in many ways. The natural assumption

---

1. While data are certainly not new, the extent and penetrations of the roles they play certainly are.
2. According to many pundits, we are many years into the Information Age. They cite various computer-related developments into the early 1980s as evidence. Closer examination suggests a subtler conclusion. The Information Technology Age, featuring stunning advances in all manner of information technology, especially microelectronics, computing, and telecommunications technology (and, by implication, the Internet) is now well along. The Information Age proper, in which organizations routinely use data and information to develop all sorts of new products and services, make better decisions, and so forth, is only now dawning.

Figure 33.1   *Accountability shifts*

in many organizations is that if it's in the computer, it must be the responsibility of the CIO. To solve this issue, organizations must recognize that finding and fixing data errors is time-consuming, expensive, non–value-added work. They must move responsibility back to original sources and, if at all possible, crystallize assignments in policy. More subtly, they must recognize the distinction between I (data and information) and IT (information technology).

- *Issue: People/organizations behave as though they owned data. Data are not shared* (Figure 33.2). Some of the more obvious aspects of the twin issues of data ownership and sharing were discussed in Chapter 31. Since many of these issues are so evident, there may be a tendency to overlook more subtle realizations of these issues. The organization must be vigilant in spotting the "quest for power" as an underlying cause of difficulties in advancing data quality.

  The 48 Laws of Power helps explain why people seem to hoard data, against the best interests of their organizations. Though not written specifically to address issues of data ownership, these laws argue persuasively that those who wish to amass personal power should amass as much data as they can and share as little as possible.

- *Issue: Unwillingness to build communications channels with customers and suppliers* (Figure 33.3). Implementing information chain and supplier management is an effective solution.

Figure 33.2   *Ownership, sharing, existing roles*

Figure 33.3   *A reluctance to engage customers and suppliers*

Figure 33.4   *Ignorance of/misunderstanding about modern principles of data quality management*

■ *Issue: Ignorance of or misconceptions about some common principles of data quality management* (Figure 33.4). Surprisingly, it never occurs to many people that data quality problems can be addressed at their sources. Another example involves people who feel that they can make up for one poor source of data by adding a second poor source. Thus, they acquire two sets of data, compare the two, and try to make corrections to the discrepancies. This almost never works. To address this issue, data quality programs must feature a heavy training and education component.

Figure 33.5   *Confusion about the role of information technology*

- *Issue: The appeal or fear of information technology and the related confusion of I (data and information) and IT (information technology)* (Figure 33.5). Related issues of organizational responsibilities have previously been discussed. Here the focus is simply on data and the computer and the feeling that new technology will solve data quality problems.

Naturally, other issues occur as well. These include the following:

- *Issue: People and organizations forget that fundamental change takes time and effort* (Figure 33.6). Many people find the points made in this book obvious and are frustrated that they are not implemented immediately. But implementing a second-generation approach to data quality virtually forces the organization to think and act differently. It takes time to change direction. A model for doing so successfully is presented in Chapter 34.

- *Issue: The word "quality" often produces negative images* (Figure 33.7).

- *Issue: Some people and organizations may wish to fight battles that cannot be won* (Figure 33.8). This issue occurs when people fail to recognize other legitimate points of view. Developing a common definition of a common term such as "customer" or "sale" is a good example.

Figure 33.6 *Failure to manage change*

Figure 33.7   *The word "quality" is associatd with negative images*

People at headquarters may recognize that opportunities to "cross-sell" or achieve efficiencies are thwarted because different departments view customers differently. One unit defines "customer" as an individual, another as all people in a "household," another as all those who live at the same address, and so on. So headquarters proposes a common definition, which is immediately rejected by the various departments. Headquarters has failed to recognize that each department's definition of "customer" has evolved to suit its business needs. It cannot win this battle without doing serious harm to the departments. Those leading the data quality effort, especially early on, must pick their spots and at the very least avoid battles that cannot be won.

Figure 33.8   *Failure to consider valid points of view*

Field Tip 33.1: Recognize that all aspects of data management, and especially data quality, have social dimensions. These soft issues can be the "hardest" to resolve.

Field Tip 33.2: Certain battles cannot be won. Avoid them.

34

Advancing the Data Culture

The social issues described in Chapter 33 are tough. But there are proactive steps that can be taken to help address them. In this chapter, we focus on three, as follows:

1.   Embrace the organization's current culture and work (most of the time) within it.

2.   Establish an appropriate relationship between data, information, and information technology.

3.   Manage change actively.

It does little good to take the stance that "unless this place changes the way it views data, nothing is ever going to get better." While the statement may well be true, it is a rather lame excuse for failure, since proactive steps are needed to make real improvements. A better approach is to recognize that all organizations have values and strengths that can be used to advance the data culture. Especially early on in the data quality program, one should not expect an organization to value data or have the skills needed to improve data quality. But the organization will have other skills and values onto which data quality can hitch a ride, as follows:

- An organization that prizes its customer focus and marketing skill, may appreciate better data quality because this enables it to know the customer a little better. And better estimates of market penetration, stemming from higher data quality, enable it to more tightly focus its marketing campaigns.

- An organization that is cost conscious may appreciate improved data quality because it reduces rework and makes costs more predictable.

- A high-technology organization may appreciate data quality because poor data cause some of the advantage gained by a technological edge to be wasted.

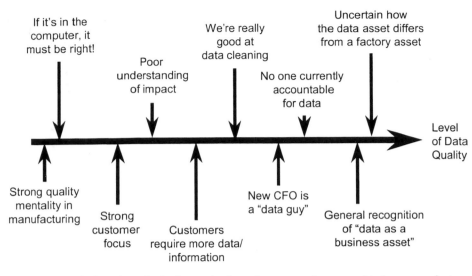

Note: This example is for a hypothetical organization—by assumption, a world-class manufacturer that recognizes that margins are thin and customers are demanding more "data/information" with products.

Figure 34.1   *Example force-field analysis of the level of data quality*

It is far easier to embed a data quality program within existing and valued activities than to start a program from scratch. Force-field analysis is a useful tool to help understand the current data culture (it is useful for many other things as well). Figure 34.1 presents the force-field analysis for a typical organization. In the figure, the line across the center of the page represents the level of data quality (it is usually the case that the level of data quality is too low). "Driving forces" are those that (can) act to increase the level of data quality, and restraining forces are those that act to decrease it. Thus, the current level of data quality resulted from a balance of the various forces pushing the level up and down. To increase the level of data quality, one can:

- Choice 1: Lessen or eliminate restraining forces and/or

- Choice 2: Strengthen or add driving forces.

One's intuition often says "Address weaknesses (that is, elect choice 1)." But choice 2, building on strength, is often more effective, as the previous examples illustrated. It is what is meant by "embracing the current culture." Best is when a single action both strengthens a driving force and lessens a restraining force.

Second, the leader should be extremely clear about the relationships between I (data) and IT (information technology). The question, "Is IT creating productivity or quality gains?" is hotly debated. We shall not join the debate here. But two points are clear:

1.   In the short term, IT (computers, communications, and data-bases) is strikingly effective at automating well-defined tasks (i.e., at implementing algorithms). It can speed things up, reduce cost, and free up people for other tasks.

2.   IT is much less effective when the task or information chain is poorly defined and/or managed.

These points lead to the conclusion that one should not apply IT to a poorly designed or managed information chain. Instead, one should first put the information chain in reasonable working order. Then automate it. This conclusion updates the quality guru's long-standing advice not to automate a manufacturing process that produced a poor product. The auto-mated process will simply produce more junk faster.

This is not to say that technology plays a subordinate role. Over the long haul, technological advances change the business landscape, lead customers to define new needs, enable people to think differently about and hence design more advanced information chains, and collect new data. Thus, the data quality leader must be alert to potentials that new technology may offer, while at the same time not expect technology to solve most data qual-ity problems. These relationships are summarized in Figure 34.2.

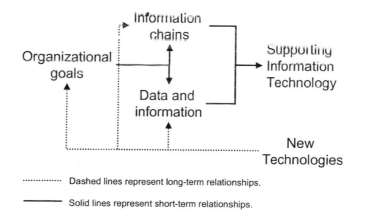

.... Dashed lines represent long-term relationships.

——— Solid lines represent short-term relationships.

Figure 34.2   *Relationships between organizations, data, information chains, and information technologies*

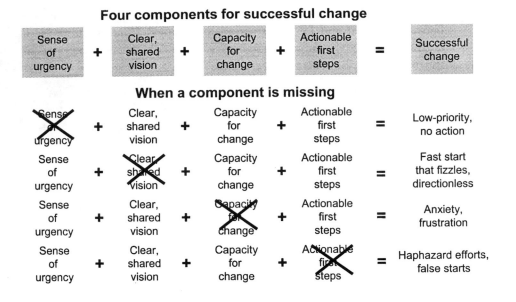

Figure 34.3   *A model for managing change*

The third way to advance the data culture is to actively manage change. Most organizations simply must change their mindset from that of finding and fixing errors to preventing them. Figure 34.3 presents a simple model for managing change. Everyone interested in data quality must have a change management paradigm and there are many good ones.[1] Figure 34.3 posits that four elements must be in place if any change is to occur. These include the following:

1.   A sense of urgency (or pressure for change). After all, as the old saying goes, "If it ain't broke, don't fix it."

2.   A clear, shared vision. People and organizations need to know where they are going.

3.   Capacity to change. Capacity to change involves several factors, including the time to work on data quality, needed financial support, and knowledge. It is usually relatively easy for most organizations to address these factors (the reader may recall that the data council was made explicitly responsible for these factors—see Chapter 30). The "emotional capacity to change" may be the most difficult. People with too much emotional energy in error detection and correction may resist change, either passively or

---

1.   Kotter, *Leading Change.* Figure 34.3, not from Kotter, is a one-diagram summary.

actively. Eventually they must be reassigned. Early on, it is impossible to distinguish those with valid concerns from those who are resisting change. Those willing to raise valid concerns are extremely important to organizations and all valid concerns should be acknowledged. Those concerns can help shape the data quality program and make it successful. But as time goes on, it may become clear that there are those who are resisting the new approach to data quality, perhaps due to some threat to their egos. While people must be given every opportunity to contribute to the data quality effort, those who subvert it cannot be tolerated. There is an old saying, of unknown origin, that applies, "Carry the wounded, but shoot the laggards."

4.   Actionable first steps. While understanding the vision is nice, people and organizations need to know what to do to get there.

To actively manage change, the leader must continually assess the penetration of these four elements across the organization, build on those that are doing well, and shore up those that are not.

Field Tip 34.1: In defining the goals of a data quality initiative, select business goals that the organization already values.

Field Tip 34.2: Recognize that data and information represent a different category asset than information technology. While they are intimately related, they must be managed separately.

Field Tip 34.3: Do not apply information technology to a poorly defined information chain. The likely result is frustration with the technology and an information chain that produces poor data faster.

Field Tip 34.4: Actively manage change.

Summaries

Two chapters conclude this book. In the last several years, recognition of the importance of and potential for high-quality data has grown enormously. And organizations are experimenting with elements of second-generation data quality systems (see Figure 15.1) other than those explained here. They are examining old issues from new perspectives. Connections between data, information, knowledge, and economic value are under intense scrutiny. Chapter 35 aims not so much to predict what will happen, but to alert the reader of some issues and opportunities that are clearly on the horizon.

The final chapter rearranges the Field Tips that close each chapter of this Field Guide. These Field Tips have been field-tested, not just on data but in manufacturing as well. Many have stood the test of time

As presented so far, each has related directly to the topic at hand, but taken together they are not organized for ready reference. Chapter 36 does so.

35

On and Just Over the Horizon

Data quality, like the Information Age, is in its infancy. We should expect it to expand and evolve in numerous directions, some predictable, some not. This chapter summarizes clear trends, even though the details are yet to emerge.

First, demands for high-quality data will grow and the demands will be fantastically diverse. We've already noted that different data customers—the employee working within an information chain, the manager, and the general public—have vastly different needs. This will accelerate.

Second, demands for new data and new information products will also grow, perhaps even faster. To date, there has been something of a commodity approach to data. Data suppliers provide pretty much the same data to everyone. But data are subtle and nuanced and even slightly different needs should motivate different data. A recent example involves the consumer price index (CPI). An issue that played out in the national news involved whether the CPI overstated inflation (a classic data quality issue). If so, government pay-outs for Social Security and other programs could accelerate much faster than desired. Part of the issue was that changing the CPI metric to better suit one purpose might compromise others.

A better approach than adjusting the CPI metric would have been to define issue-specific CPIs. Thus, if one program's goal is to adjust seniors' income so they are not left out, there should be a "senior-CPI" specially crafted to meet the needs of that program and its constituencies. The market basket used in calculating this CPI would reflect seniors' purchases, not those of the general public. If medical expenses consume a larger share of seniors' budgets and medical costs are rising faster, then the "senior-CPI" will reflect this.

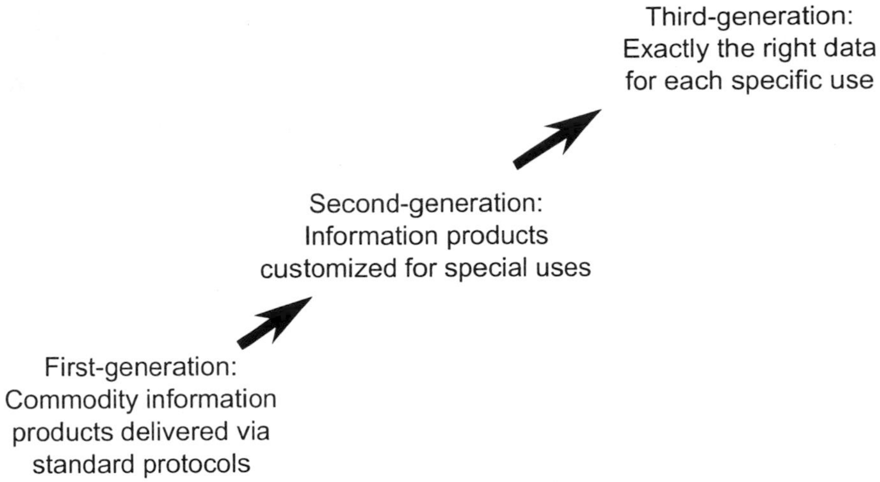

Third-generation:
Exactly the right data
for each specific use

Second-generation:
Information products
customized for special uses

First-generation:
Commodity information
products delivered via
standard protocols

Figure 35.1   *Data products will evolve from commodities to fit the needs of each specific use*

On the other hand, those who manage the money supply may be more concerned about changes in the CPI than in the actual number. For their purposes, the CPI may be just fine.

A similar discussion holds for the census and numerous other metrics and data sets. The point of this discussion is not to single out the Department of Commerce, the Census Bureau, or the federal government. Rather it is to illustrate an important trend, and the CPI and Census Bureau may be the most familiar examples. The trend is away from commodity data and information products and toward exactly the right data to support each specific purpose. Figure 35.1 summarizes this trend. The fundamentals of mass customization may well provide the needed insights for doing so.

Third, we expect quality to extend to information and knowledge. Indeed, "knowledge management" has acquired a certain cachet in recent years. Strictly speaking, this *Field Guide* concerns data, but there is good reason to believe that the techniques presented apply to information and knowledge as well. Part of the challenge will be to determine what information and knowledge are. Though data are intangible, they are structured. This helps one translate and extend the principles of quality science, as developed for the very tangible world of manufacturing, to data. There is less agreement on definitions of information and knowledge. This issue will have to be resolved.

The next item on the horizon is a long battle over privacy. To quote an unknown source, "Privacy will be to the Information Age what safety was to the Industrial Age." Some argue that product safety has gone too far. It does seem extreme that a cup of coffee must bear the label "Caution—Contents may be hot." But in the end, protection of the consumer has earned primacy.

The trend seems to be in the opposite direction regarding privacy (in the United States anyway), with more and more personal data being used for more and more purposes beyond what the consumer agreed to or expected. It is impossible to determine whether the current trend will continue or the longer-term trend of consumer protection—and hence government policy to define and protect consumers' rights to privacy—will win out.

The cautious (and perhaps the prudent) will go to great lengths to assure their customers that they will not use data for purposes other than those the customer explicitly permits. The more aggressive will use data about customers any way they can. Those adopting a middle ground will not sell customer data. But they will feel free to use those data for internal purposes.

Whichever approach an organization adopts, it must make its privacy policy explicit, communicate its policy to customers in no uncertain terms, and adhere to it without fail.

The fifth trend involves the further development of data markets. There are relatively few data and information products on the open market compared with the fantastic array of manufactured goods. Nor are data markets well developed. Since data customer needs are growing, one should expect many more data vendors (distinct from software or service vendors) to fill these gaps. There are a few markets where this is already occurring. For example, a number of data vendors try to fill the data needs of the financial services industry.

It is evident that the quantity, diversity, and richness of data acquired, stored, networked, and used will continue to grow at enormous rates. Despite the impressive growth in database, networking, bandwidth, and data analysis capabilities, technological issues are not yet solved.

Our final observation is that organizational forms must evolve to better utilize data as resources. The so-called command and control structure grew up to meet the information processing needs of the large organizations of the day—railroads, armies, and governments. Most data and information flowed up and down the organizational chart. So organizational structure was perfectly appropriate.

But most data flows are no longer up and down. Data flow across department and organizational boundaries in both predictable and seemingly chaotic fashions. Most management, on the other hand, is still up and down. So today organizational structure and information flow are mis-aligned. There is no simple solution as yet to resolve this misalignment.

Field Tip 35.1: Data that were of exceptionally high quality yesterday are of acceptable quality today and will be of unacceptable quality tomorrow.

Field Tip 35.2: Seek exactly the right data for each purpose.

Field Tip 35.3: Treat privacy seriously. At the very least, inform all customers (not just Internet customers) of your privacy policy and adhere to it.

Field Tip 35.4: Keep current on information technologies. The issues can only grow more difficult.

Field Tips Reorganized

A total of seventy-one field tips have concluded chapters of this *Field Guide.* Sixteen have been selected as the most important, useful, or frequently used and are presented for ready reference in Figure 36.1.

Similarly, several themes recur. So this chapter reorganizes the field tips according to several subjects. Within each subject, tips have been reorganized for reading top to bottom. A few tips are included in two or more subject areas. The subjects include the following:

- *Business case for data quality:* Many field tips have emphasized the need to create business opportunity and/or solve the most important business problems through data quality. See Figure 36.2.

- *Customers:* Many field tips reflect the essential role played by customers, especially the need to understand that there are many data customers with different needs. See Figure 36.3.

- *Managing and improving data quality:* Many field tips discuss the various aspects of making improvements. These range from the nuts and bolts of completing improvement projects to managerial responsibility. See Figure 36.4.

- *Social issues:* The difficult issues in data quality are social, not technical. Many field tips aim to help recognize and/or deal with these. See Figure 36.5.

- *Suppliers:* Most organizations receive a great deal of data from outside. These data must be included in the data quality program. See Figure 36.6.

- *Technology:* Some people think that "since data are stored in computers, they must be the responsibility of the IT department" (a social issue). Many field tips aim to recognize the proper roles for technology in a data quality program. See Figure 36.7.

- *Nature of data:* Some field tips recognize unique properties of data as business assets. See Figure 36.8.

Field Tip 1.1: An organization's most senior leader must not delegate responsibility for data quality. The losses due to poor quality are simply too great. Fortunately, high-quality data earns enormous returns.

Field Tip 6.1: Anyone who either uses or creates data must be concerned about their quality. No one is left out. No one in any industry nor government. No one at any level of management. No job category. And the impact of data quality is just as great in private life as well.

Field Tip 31.1: The First Principle of Data Quality Management: Assign responsibility for the quality of data to those who create them. If this is not possible, assign responsibility as close to data creation as possible.

Field Tip 13.1: First, *prevent future errors, then clean up existing errors.* Unless circumstances are dire, resist efforts to compromise on this point.

Field Tip F.1: Data are either created inside the organization or obtained from outside. Apply supplier management to data obtained from outside and information chain management created inside.

Field Tip 33.1: Recognize that all aspects of data management, and especially data quality have social dimensions. These "soft" issues can be the "hardest" to resolve.

Field Tip 14.1: Data are only of high quality if those who use them say so. Usually high-quality data must both be free of defects and possess features that customers need.

Field Tip 17.2: As a practical matter, data quality involves meeting the most important needs of the most important customers. Be prepared to make the tough choices.

Field Tip 16.1: To improve quality, first implement effective requirements and feedback channels with customers and suppliers.

Field Tip 22.1: Don't underestimate the simple elegance of quality improvement. Other than teamwork, training, and discipline, it requires no special skills. Anyone who wants to can be an effective contributor.

Field Tip 22.4: Poor training and/or communication of requirements lie at the root of many data quality problems. They are relatively easy to fix.

Field Tip 9.1: In developing the case for data quality, demonstrate how improvements will lead to competitive advantage.

Field Tip 2.1: The Internet is virgin territory for data quality. Dot.coms will need to establish trust with consumers. Those that provide high-quality data have a better chance of doing so and can expect to achieve competitive advantages. Those who don't may be disadvantaged.

Field Tip 15.1: Do not underestimate how strongly individuals and organizations will cling to their beliefs in data clean-up. And don't be misled—clean-up is non–value-added work.

Field Tip 34.2: Recognize that data and information represent a different asset category than information technology. While they are intimately related, they must be managed separately.

Field Tip 34.3: Do not apply information technology to a poorly defined information chain. The likely result is frustration with the technology and an information chain that produces poor data faster.

Figure 36.1   *Most important field tips*

Field Tip 9.1: In developing the case for data quality, demonstrate how improvements will lead to competitive advantage.

Field Tip 34.1: In defining the goals of a data quality initiative, select business goals that the organization already values.

Field Tip 3.1: Look for opportunities to improve data quality "where the money is." Billing is a natural. Many organizations find that they can reduce "underbilling" for little added cost.

Field Tip 8.1: Most Important data quality problems don't present themselves as such. Identify them through their impact on the organization's most important business objectives.

Field Tip 7.1: One goal of the data quality program should be to prevent embarrassment, both personal or organizational, both internally or publicly.

Field Tip 4.1: The most important data are those required for executing the most important strategies.

Field Tip 12.1: All data quality programs should focus first on the most important data

Field Tip 27.2: Recognize that a Department's efforts to find and correct data received from upstream is non–value-added work and adds time and expense. For the most important information chains, information chain management is the technique of choice for minimizing this non–value-added work.

Field Tip 10.1: Don't be misled. Finding and correcting errors is non–value-added work. It is difficult, expensive, and time consuming as well. Most importantly, it doesn't work very well.

Field Tip 18.3: Use examples to illustrate results. But do not confuse an anecdote with a compelling case for action.

Field Tip 12.3: If funds are tight, make the data quality effort self funding. A useful first step is to quit creating and/or acquiring data that are never used.

Figure 36.2   *Field tips for building the business case for data quality*

Field Tip 17.1: Determining customer needs is unbelievably hard work. But there is no substitute for doing so. And the rewards are great.

Field Tip 17.2: As a practical matter, data quality involves meeting the most important needs of the most important customers. Be prepared to make the tough choices.

Field Tip 28.1: Managers have an insatiable need for high-quality data. Their needs are quite distinct from operational needs, but the techniques to satisfy them are exactly the same.

Field Tip 14.1: Data are only of high quality if those who use them say so. Usually high-quality data must both be free of defects and possess features that customers need.

Field Tip 17.3: You can't reasonably expect data customers to develop detailed requirements. Instead, work with them to figure out how they use data and their needs. Data sources must translate those needs into requirements.

Field Tip 35.1: Data that were of exceptionally high quality yesterday are of acceptable quality tomorrow and will be of unacceptable quality tomorrow.

Field Tip 35.2: Seek exactly the right data for each purpose.

Field Tip 16.1: To improve quality, first implement effective requirements and feedback channels with customers and suppliers.

Field Tip 35.3: Treat privacy seriously. At the very least, inform all customers (not just Internet customers) of your privacy policy and adhere to it.

Field Tip 18.1: Before taking measurements of data quality levels, first think through how the customers of the results should use them.

Field Tip 18.2: Present results in simple, compelling formats. Emphasize not just the error rate, but the impact on the organization.

Field Tip 2.1: The Internet is virgin territory for data quality. Dot.coms will need to establish trust with consumers. Those that provide high-quality data have a better chance of doing so and can expect to achieve competitive advantages. Those who don't may be disadvantaged.

Figure 36.3   *Field tips that bear on customers*

Field Tip 1.1: An organization's most senior leader must not delegate responsibility for data quality. The losses due to poor quality are simply too great. Fortunately, high-quality data earns enormous returns.

Field Tip 6.1: Anyone who either uses or creates data must be concerned about their quality. No one is left out. No one in any industry nor government. No one at any level of management. No job category. And the impact of data quality is just as great in private life as well.

Field Tip 31.1: The First Principle of Data Quality Management: Assign responsibility for the quality of data to those who create them. If this is not possible, assign responsibility as close to data creation as possible.

Figure 36.4   *Field tips for managing and improving data quality*

Field Tip 13.1: First, *prevent future errors, then clean up existing errors.* Unless circumstances are dire, resist efforts to compromise on this point.

Field Tip 30.1: For maximum impact, senior management must lead data quality efforts. Senior managers who eschew their data responsibilities seem not to understand the importance of data and information in the Information Age.

Field Tip F.1: Data are either created inside the organization or obtained from outside. Apply supplier management to data obtained from outside and apply process management created inside.

Field Tip 27.1: Recognize that data flows horizontally across the organization. The most important such "flows" should be explicitly managed as information chains.

Field Tip 27.4: To start, identify a few critical information chains and form a (senior) cross-functional team to manage the chain end-to-end.

Field Tip 16.1: To improve quality, first implement effective requirements and feedback channels with customers and suppliers.

Field Tip 19.1: Data tracking is the measurement vehicle of choice when detailed, in-chain measurements of data accuracy and cycle time are needed.

Field Tip 20.1: Just because data have "passed the edits," does not ensure that the data are of acceptable quality.

Field Tip 20.2: Data editing should be employed (as part of a larger data quality program) to prevent errors from causing damage downstream.

Field Tip 21.1: Use control charts to establish a technical basis for preventing errors. First establish control. Then make improvements to meet customer requirements.

Field Tip 22.1: Don't underestimate the simple elegance of quality improvement. Other than teamwork, training, and discipline, it requires no special skills. Anyone who wants to can be an effective contributor.

Field Tip 22.2: Get in the habit of continuous improvement. Set and meet simple goals, like "complete a project every month."

Field Tip 23.1: Demand aggressive rates of improvement.

Field Tip 24.3: Design new information chains to facilitate continuous improvement.

Field Tip 25.1: At its heart, re-engineering is about data. So re-engineering teams should apply principles of good data quality design from the start.

Field Tip 5.2: Implement an end-to-end *data resource chain* to ensure that data resource data are well-defined, kept up-to-date, and made easily available to all. Implement *data modeling* and *standards* chains as support.

Field Tip 5.3: Begin, not by "cleaning up" inadequate data resource data, but by implementing the data resource chain.

Field Tip 5.4: Build data quality into a data warehouse. One way to do so is to name a "warehouse supplier manager," who functions much like any other data supplier manager.

Figure 36.4   *Field tips for managing and improving data quality (continued)*

Field Tip 33.1: Recognize that all aspects of data management, and especially data quality have social dimensions. These "soft" issues can be the "hardest" to resolve.

Field Tip 34.4: Actively manage change.

Field Tip 32.1: Managing data quality is hard enough without organizational mischief. So overlay the needed structures for leadership and support, process and supplier management, and all projects on the existing organization chart.

Field Tip 31.2: Data ownership is a "slippery slope." On paper, the concept makes good sense, but it presents dangers. Managers and departments must have specific accountabilities and rights, but they cannot own data.

Field Tip 27.3: In most cases, it will be middle managers who most tenaciously resist process management because it most impacts their jobs.

Field Tip 28.2: Manage decision making like any other information chain.

Field Tip 22.4: Poor training and/or communication of requirements lie at the root of many data quality problems. They are relatively easy to fix.

Field Tip 22.3: Carefully define most projects to be small and achievable by a small team of people in a short amount of time.

Field Tip 33.2: Certain "battles" cannot be won. Avoid them.

Field Tip 4.2: Business units arrive at different definitions of "customer" because they run their businesses differently.

Field Tip 4.3: Getting business units to agree on a common definition is almost impossible. Recognize legitimate business needs and develop data structures to meet them.

Field Tip 15.1: Do not underestimate how strongly individuals and organizations will cling to their beliefs in data clean-up. And don't be misled—clean-up is non–value-added work.

Figure 36.5   *Field tips for recognizing and handling social issues*

Field Tip 5.1: Insist that data suppliers provide and keep data resource data current.

Field Tip 26.1: A good area to start the data quality program is with critical data suppliers.

Field Tip 24.2: Emphasize communication of requirements to those expected to meet them.

Field Tip 26.2: Most data suppliers want to provide high-quality data and are in dire need of good requirements. The leaders, those who first articulate clear requirements and keep them current, are almost always heard.

Field Tip 26.3: Data supplier managers should be named and held accountable for advancing the supplier management cycle.

Field Tip 26.5: Within the organization, it is often appropriate to apply supplier management to the other departments on which one depends.

Field Tip 24.1: Several original data sources may be required to meet a customer's need. Deploy appropriate requirements to each source.

Field Tip 26.4: "Partnership" may be the most over-used phrase in business lingo. Reserve it for those few suppliers on whom you absolutely depend.

Figure 36.6   *Field tips for supplier data quality*

Field Tip 34-2: Recognize that data and information represent a different asset category than information technology. While they are intimately related, they must be managed separately.

Field Tip 24.4: Design information chains first, then supporting information technology.

Field Tip 34.3: Do not apply information technology to a poorly defined information chain. The likely result is frustration with the technology and an information chain that produces poor data faster.

Field Tip 5.5: Allow ample time for data quality in front of the warehouse effort. Warehouse customers and their needs are new and meeting them requires many sources to do their parts.

Field Tip 11.1: Don't be seduced by the glamour of fancy tools to clean-up erred data. They may help in the short term but, over the long haul, there is no substitute for preventing errors.

Field Tip 29.1: It is almost always better to pick specific tools to solve specific problems than to pick general tools to solve general problems.

Field Tip 35.4. Keep current on information technologies. The issues can only grow more difficult.

Figure 36.7   *Field tips on the role of technology*

Field Tip 34.2: Recognize that data and information represent a different asset category than information technology. While they are intimately related, they must be managed separately.

Field Tip 27.1: Recognize that data flows horizontally across the organization. The most important such "flows" should be explicitly managed as information chains.

Field Tip 12.2: The "rate of new data creation" is the most important factor in determining the best approach to data quality.

Figure 36.8   *Field tips on the nature of data*

Appendix: The United States Elections of 2000

As *Data Quality: The Field Guide* winds its way into publication, the nation, indeed the entire world, is again captivated by issues of poor data quality. The elections in the United States have taken place and the results are unfolding. And in the most important election of all, for President of the United States, we still (as of November 15, 2000) do not know who the winner will be. Of course, some votes are as yet uncounted. But the wait for those votes is not what has captured the world's attention. Rather it is questions of:

- The accuracy of the various counts and recounts
- How the end-to-end "election chain" is supposed to work
- The final result and the consequences of the above

People everywhere must now understand that data quality is not some esoteric computer issue, but one that can affect their daily lives in profound ways. Somewhat more subtly, most people, whether they support or oppose recounts, realize how hard they are to complete. *The Field Guide* has repeatedly hammered home the message that data quality efforts must focus on preventing future errors. Obviously, the period until the next election offers the opportunity to do so.

Volumes will be written about all aspects of the elections in many states. Intense scrutiny will be the norm. We do not wish to join the debate (we noted earlier in *The Field Guide* that everything about data quality was politically charged. At the time that statement was written we did not know how timely it was). We do, however, wish to summarize a few points that those who scrutinize elections in the hope of preventing future errors should find pertinent.[1] In some way or another, all components of second-generation data quality systems must be brought to bear.[2] First, the end-to-

---

1. We do not consider purely political issues, such as whether the Electoral College should be abolished.

end "election chain"[3] is long and complex. It involves many steps, from voter registration, to design of ballots, to providing absentee ballots, to qualifying voters, to collecting actual votes, to setting standards (what is a "legitimate vote," for example), to tabulating and counting votes at precincts, to aggregating them to the state level, and so forth. Errors appear to have occurred at every step and possibly between many. The entire election chain, not simply individual components, must be scrutinized. In particular, attention should focus first on the end-to-end chain, then on the individual steps, and finally on possible technological improvements.

Second, it is probably true, as noted in *The New York Times*, that most issues are rooted in a lack of attention more than anything else. This point underscores the need for leadership at all levels; national, state, and county. Further, state laws codify the requirements that those who run elections must meet. In the lingo of data quality, these are the customer requirements. But the requirements are out-of-date, confusing, and contradictory in many cases. In many respects politicians have no one to blame but themselves. State governing bodies must take responsibility for clarifying their requirements.

Third, with a few possible exceptions, the quality of year 2000 elections was no worse than the quality of past elections. Those responsible for past elections seem not to have received feedback that would motivate them to correct deficiencies. Feedback channels must be built into future election chains to facilitate continuous improvement. For example, while it is likely that the 2004 elections will be better, it is extremely unlikely that they will be perfect. The spirit of further improvement for 2008, 2112, etc., is critical. And it will be necessary to write laws that codify not just what must happen next time, but with an eye towards these future improvements.

Fourth, there is some evidence that "hand recounts" are less accurate than machine recounts, at least in Florida. This is consistent with observations made throughout *The Field Guide* that finding and fixing errors is very difficult. Similarly, many voters are upset that their votes were invalidated because they mistakenly voted twice. Every effort must be made to design the new chain so that hand recounts will not be necessary. For example, ballots should be validated immediately. A voter should be advised that his or her vote is invalid and be given the opportunity to correct it *before he or she leaves the polling place.*

---

2.   We will post updates with *The Field Guide*'s figures and tables from time to time (See Instructions for Downloading Figures and Tables).

3.   For our purposes here, an election chain is considered within a state.

Fifth, it will be very important to measure election quality against customer requirements. Virtually everyone agrees that "fairness" and "accuracy" are important. Translating these requirements into measures will be difficult, but it is absolutely essential. To illustrate, consider accuracy. Measures of accuracy will be of the form:

$$accuracy \equiv \frac{properly\ counted\ votes}{total\ votes}$$

But there are problems. How do we "count" the following:

- A voter who is turned away from a polling place
- An invalid ballot (like the double-punched ballots in Florida)
- A voter who requests, but does not receive, an absentee ballot

This list can go on and on. This list illustrates a further point about the need for standards. Some of the bitterest battles appear to be over mundane issues (does a "hanging chad" count?) for which standards are needed.

Election quality measurements should, of course, be made public. In experimenting using numbers reported in *The New York Times* and on CNN.com, I obtained measures of accuracy ranging from 88% to 99.9% It may be difficult to separate the facts from visceral reactions to the facts. For example 88% "sounds pretty bad" and 99.9% "sounds pretty good" (Impressive as 99.9% sounds, it still means that 100,000 votes may have been erroneously counted). But the focus on improvement is more important than the emotional response to a number.

Finally, the "customers" of elections cannot reasonably expect counts to be perfect. But they can demand immediate and continual improvement. For the next Presidential election, they should demand at least an order of magnitude improvement.

Little Silver, NJ
November 15, 2000

Glossary

accuracy Almost always one of the most important dimensions of data quality. Defined as a measure of the degree of agreement between a data value or collection of data values and a source agreed to be correct. Informally customers say they need "data to be accurate" and mean they require that data values agree with the real-world.

appropriate use An often-important dimension of data quality. Since data may be used for many things, many customers desire that sources indicate which uses the data supports. To illustrate, it may be perfectly appropriate to use a person's age in making a pension calculation, but inappropriate (even illegal) to use that same datum in a hiring decision.

attribute The element of a datum that defines a property of the entity. For example, the attribute in the data triple <Thomas C. Redman, Sex, M> is "Sex." See "datum" for a definition of a datum.

availability An important dimension of data quality. Availability is a measure of the degree to which needed data may be easily acquired by a data customer. Availability is particularly important to a data customer that purchases or otherwise acquires data from a data supplier. Such customers expect "the data to be available for use when expected."

business rule A constraint on the values that data may take. For example, the attribute "Sex" may take only two values: M (for male) and F (for female). Another somewhat more involved example involves the rules that make up the so-called postal standard. Certain addresses, such as "New York City, New York 90210" are not permitted because they fail rules in the postal standard. Business rules can be quite complex, involving many attributes.

clean-up (database) A special activity aimed at identifying and correcting errors in data values already stored (in a database).

clear definition   An important dimension of data quality. A datum is clearly defined if it is unambiguously defined using simple terms.

common cause   In statistical quality control, a source of variation within or internal to a process or information chain. In everyday use, common cause refers to a root cause of error that underlies many errors. As an example, a poorly trained clerk may be the common cause of many data errors in a particular field.

completeness   An important dimension of data quality. Completeness is a measure of the degree to which data values are present for required attributes or the degree to which required data records are present. Conversely, "missing data attributes" or "missing data records" mean the data are incomplete.

comprehensiveness   An important dimension of data quality. Technically, comprehensiveness measures whether a collection of data is sufficient for a customer to complete a given task. Importantly, comprehensiveness depends on the task at hand—a collection of data may well be sufficient to make one decision and not another.

consistency   An important dimension of data quality. Technically, consistency is a measure of the degree to which a set of data satisfies business rules. As a simple example, two data values are consistent if they do not disagree. For a given entity, AREA CODE = 212 (New York City) and ZIP CODE = 90210 (Hollywood, CA) (almost certainly, though there are exceptions) violate a business rule and so are inconsistent.

control   Also "in-control." In statistical quality control, this is a state achieved when evidence indicates the absence of a special cause of variation. Equivalently, the evidence suggests that future performance is predictable, within limits. In modern data quality management, the goal is to prevent future errors. Thus the ability to predict future performance is important.

control chart   A graphical device for determining whether a process or information chain is in control. For data quality, one most often uses a "p-chart," which features a time series plot of the error rate, a Center Line, an Upper Control Limit, and a Lower Control Limit. See Figure 21.2.

currency   An important dimension of data quality. Currency is a measure of the degree to which data values are up-to-date. Data values that are not current are referred to as "out-of-date."

customer-supplier model   A model of a process or information chain emphasizing the interfaces between suppliers, the chain, and customers. One type of interface involves data flow from supplier to customer. The other interfaces involve customer requirements and feedback. See Figure 16.1.

cycle time   The end-to-end time required for a process or information chain to complete a work item.

data   Any collection of datum. Note that we use "datum" as the singular and "data" as the plural. See "datum."

database   A formal, usually computerized, collection of data.

data council   The management body charged with leading the data quality program. Senior leadership and support has proven an essential ingredient to successful data quality programs, probably because most of the important issues are of a cross-organizational nature. In principle, the required leadership and support may be provided by a single, well-placed individual. But in practice it is most often a senior team that provides this leadership.

data model   Since the real-world is so messy, we (mankind) develop simple models to help us understand it (the real-world). There are many kinds of such models (linear models, mathematical models, flowcharts, etc.). A data model captures pertinent features of the real-world in data. Different organizations employ different models to suit their ends. Thus the Internal Revenue Service models people as "taxpayers," employers model the same people as "employees," and businesses model them as "customers."

data policy   A statement that delineates management responsibilities for data and for activities that touch and/or impact data and information. The best policies aim to hold data sources accountable for the quality of data they create.

data quality   The degree to which data meet the specific needs of specific customers. Note that one customer may find data to be of high quality (for one use of the data), while another finds the same data to be of low quality (for another use).

data resource data   Data about the data. Sometimes called metadata. Data resource data may define what data mean, how they can be accessed, how frequently they are updated, how one may obtain help, etc.

(data) supplier management   A set of specific, repeatable tasks for managing external suppliers of data. Data supplier management builds needed communications channels so suppliers understand what is expected and helps suppliers make needed improvements to close performance gaps. See Chapter 26.

data tracking   A technique for measuring the data accuracy and the cycle time associated with an information chain. See Chapter 19.

data value   Technically, the element of a datum that specifies an element of the domain assigned to the specified attribute. As an example, the "M" in <Thomas C. Redman, Sex, M>. In everyday usage, people often use the term "data" to refer to the data value. See datum.

data warehouse   An electronic database usually organized to support decision-making. In decision-making, one must often access large amounts of data. Contrast with a transactional database, which is organized to support access of a relatively small amount of data in real-time.

datum   A triple <entity, attribute, value>. As a simple example, <Thomas C. Redman, Sex, M> is interpreted to refer to the entity which is the author, the attribute "Sex" and "M" (or male). In everyday use, one says "Thomas C. Redman's Sex is Male."

define a view   Another name for the data modeling chain. Specifically in data modeling, one takes (i.e., defines) a particular view of the real-world to be captured in data.

domain   In a datum, <entity, attribute, value>, the value element may take on certain permitted values. The domain defines this set of permitted values. Thus in <Person, Sex, value>, the attribute Sex may assume one of two values: M (male) or F (female). Thus (M, F) is the domain for the Sex attribute.

early warning   An important dimension of data quality, especially to customers of data supplied by external suppliers. Customers may need to be advised in advance if a set of data will not arrive as expected or do not meet quality requirements.

ease of interpretation   An important dimension of data quality. Data are easy to interpret if the data customer can easily understand what they mean. Ease of interpretation is closely related to clear definition.

edit   A (usually computerized) routine that tests a business rule on a set of data.

entity The element of a datum that refers to a specific individual or instance in the real-world. The "Thomas C. Redman" in <Thomas C. Redman, Sex, M>. See datum.

flowchart A model of a process or information chain that emphasizes the sequence of work activities. The flowchart is usually presented pictorially.

format A specified set of rules for presenting and/or storing data.

help An important (and sometimes overlooked) dimension of data quality. "Help" is the ability to get and receive aid to better use data.

histogram In quality improvement, a bar chart in which categories of error are plotted on the *x*-axis and the frequency (percentage) is plotted on the *y*-axis.

identifiability An important property of data quality. A good data model calls for each distinct entity to be uniquely identified (so they are not confused with one another). This property is called identifiability. Importantly, when asked about their data requirements, few customers will specify identifiability—the concept is just so basic that it does not occur to them that this property would not be provided.

in-control Or simply "control." In statistical quality control, this is a state achieved when evidence indicates the absence of a special cause of variation. Equivalently, evidence suggests that future performance is predictable, within limits. See Chapter 21.

information chain The portions of a large, cross-functional process that involve data and information. Information chains are the means by which organizations create new data and managing them is critical to achieving high-quality data. See "process."

information chain management cycle a set of specific, repeatable tasks for defining a process or information chain, understanding customers' needs, establishing control, and making improvements. Since information chains are the means by which organizations create new data, managing them is critical to achieving high-quality data. See Chapter 27.

information chain management team A group assembled by the information chain owner to assist him or her in carrying out information chain management. Since many information chains cross organizational boundaries and each step is highly technical, the information chain owner assembles this team to provide the needed cross-organizational expertise and coordination.

information chain owner   The person responsible for end-to-end information chain performance. The person is assumed to have authority to make changes.

measurement   (In this context) The process of objectively determining how well an information chain or data supplier is performing with respect to dimensions of data quality and/or requirements.

metadata   Data about data. The more modern name is data resource data. Metadata help a data customer understand what data mean, gain access, etc.

pareto chart   In quality improvement, a bar chart in which categories on the x-axis are ordered by the height of the bars plotted on the y-axis (frequency, percentage, etc.). The leftmost categories represent the greatest opportunity for improvement.

process   A set of interrelated work activities, usually characterized by specific inputs and repeated value-added steps, which produce a specific set of outputs.

project   A defined activity for carrying out a selected improvement opportunity (see Chapter 22). Note the contrast between "information chain" (or "process") which is managed continuously and "project," which is managed to completion.

redundancy   The state of having multiple copies of data.

relevancy   An important dimension of data quality. Data are relevant to a particular task or decision if they contribute to the completion of that task or making of the decision.

requirements   Customer-derived definitions of what is expected of an information chain or data supplier.

security   An important dimension of data quality. Data are secure if the risk of data being lost and/or stolen is low. Note that "risk" includes both the probability of loss/theft and the consequences of the loss/theft. Thus, if the probability that data are lost is low, but the consequence is high, the risk is still high.

source   An important dimension of data quality. Like customers of other products and services, data customers come to trust some sources of data as of consistently high quality (and perhaps to mistrust others). So they want to know the source(s) of data they use.

special cause In statistical quality control, a source of variation external to the information chain. For example, a new release of software supporting some step in an information chain may introduce new errors. A control chart helps the information chain owner identify and remedy this "cause" quickly.

stable (information chain) An information chain or process in a state of control. See "control."

statistical quality control (SQC) Also called statistical process control (SPC). A technique for measuring information chain or process performance, determining whether special causes are present, and taking appropriate action. In data quality management, we also compare performance against customer requirements. See Chapter 21.

(data) supplier management A set of specific, repeatable tasks for managing external suppliers of data. Data supplier management builds needed communications channels so suppliers understand what is expected and helps suppliers make needed improvements to close performance gaps. See Chapter 26.

timeliness An important measure of data quality. Timeliness is a measure of the degree to which an information chain or process is completed within a prespecified date or time. Timeliness is related to currency—data are current if they are up-to-date and are the usual result of a timely information chain.

tracked record In data tracking, a data record tagged during the first step of an information chain or process for further analysis. See Chapter 19.

unit cost A important dimension of data quality. Unit cost is the cost per data record. Sometimes a base unit other than data record is used. Data customers often express the need to keep costs down. In some management circles, cost and quality are managed separately. The point of view taken here is that unit cost is like any other dimension of data quality and all should be managed simultaneously.

value (data) In a datum, the element that specifies the member of the domain assigned to the <entity, attribute> pair. The "M" in <Thomas C. Redman, Sex, M>.

References

Brackett, Michael H., *Data Sharing*, New York: John Wiley & Sons, 1994.

Brown, John Seely, and Duguid, Paul, *The Social Life of Information*, Boston: Harvard Business School Press, 2000.

Davenport, Thomas H., *Information Ecology*, New York: Oxford University Press, 1997.

Davenport, Thomas H., *Process Innovation*, Boston: Harvard Business School Press, 1993

Deming, W. Edwards, *Quality, Productivity, and Competitive Position*, Cambridge: MIT CAES, 1982.

Drucker, Peter F., *Management*, New York: Harper & Row, 1985.

English, Larry P., *Improving Data Warehouse and Business Information Quality*, New York: John Wiley & Sons, 1999.

Evans, Philip, and Wurster, Thomas S., *Blown to Bits*, Boston: Harvard Business School Press, 2000.

Follett, Mary Parker, *Prophet of Management*, Boston: Harvard Business School Press, 1995.

Goldratt, Eliyahu M., and Cox, Jeff, *The Goal, A Process of Ongoing Improvement*, Croton-On-Hudson: North River Press, 1986.

Grant, Eugene L., and Leavenworth, Richard S., *Statistical Quality Control, Sixth Edition*, New York: McGraw-Hill, 1988.

Greene, Robert, and Elffers, Joost, *The 48 Laws of Power*, New York: Viking Press, 1998.

Hammer, Michael, *Beyond Reengineering*, New York: Harper Business, 1996.

Huang, Kuan-Tsae, Lee, Yang W., and Wang, Richard Y., *Quality Information and Knowledge*, Upper Saddle River: Prentice Hall PTR, 1999.

Juran, J. M., *Managerial Breakthrough*, New York: McGraw-Hill, 1964.

Kent, William, *Data and Reality*, Amsterdam: North-Holland Publishing Co., 1978.

Klien, Gary, *Sources of Power: How People Make Decisions*, Cambridge, MA: MIT Press, 1998.

Kotter, John P., *Leading Change*, Boston: Harvard Business School Press, 1996.

Landauer, Thomas K., *The Trouble with Computers*, Boston: MIT Press, 1997.

McGregor, Douglas, *The Human Side of Enterprise*, New York: McGraw-Hill, 1985.

Redman, Thomas C., *Data Quality for the Information Age*, Boston: Artech House, 1996.

Ross, Ronald G., *The Business Rule Book*, Boston: Database Research Group, Inc., 1997

Planck, Max, *Scientific Autobiography and Other Papers,* New York: Philosophical Library, 1949.

Shapiro, Carl, and Varian, Hal R., *Information Rules*, Boston: Harvard Business School Press, 1999.

Shewhart, Walter A., *Statistical Method from the Viewpoint of Quality Control*, Mineola: Dover Publications, 1986

Strassmann, Paul A., *The Politics of Information Management*, New Canaan: The Information Economics Press, 1995.

Taylor, Frederick Winslow, *The Principles of Scientific Management*, Mineola: Dover Publications, 1998.

Treacy, Michael, and Wiersema, Fred, *The Discipline of Market Leaders*, New York: Addison Wesley, 1995.

Instructions for Downloading Figures and Tables

1. Point your browser to the Butterworth-Heinemann Web site:
   www.husa.com/digitalpress

2. Locate *Data Quality: The Field Guide* and click on the title next to the picture. ⟶

3. Click the "Download Figures and Tables" link.

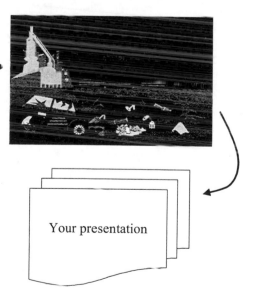

4. Find the figure you want. ⟶

5. Download it.

6. Cut and paste it into your presentation.

Your presentation

Other Books by Thomas C. Redman, Ph.D.

Data Quality: Management and Technology, Bantam Books, 1992

Data Quality for the Information Age, Artech, 1996

Index

48 Laws of Power, 190

B

Background, 69–97
Balanced scorecard, 172
Billing, 15–19
  biased, 44
  chain, 17, 18
  desired quality system for, 18
  issues, 15, 44
  overbilling, 16–17
  quality system for, 16
  unbiased, 16–17, 44
  underbilling, 16, 19
Bivariate domains, 119
Business case, 37–49
  building, 48–49
  competitive advantage and, 47–49
  disasters and, 39–41
  DQS element, 80
  field tips for building, 211
  poor data quality and, 43–46

C

CEOs, 3–5
  concerns, 5
  data quality delegation and, 5
  data quality demand and, 5
  identification as, 35
  poor data quality and, 3–4

superior data quality and, 4
  See also Senior leadership
Certification program, 157–58
  defined, 157
  elements, 157
  illustrated, 158
  See also Supplier management
Change
  capacity for, 200–201
  elements for, 200–201
  management model, 200
  time/effort of, 193
Chief financial officers, 15
  data quality and, 15
  identification with, 35
  See also Senior leadership
Chief Information Officers (CIOs), 27–34
  data quality concerns, 27–28
  data quality improvement, 32–33
  as data source, 32
  data uses, 27
  data warehouses and, 31–32
  opportunity, 33
  trap, 33
  See also Senior leadership
Clean-up
  beliefs, 78
  conclusions, 57
  costs, 60
  error prevention before, 65–66

Clean-up *(cont'd.)*
    methods, 54–55, 57
    not repeating, 66
    not using, 65
    paradigm, 76
    quality levels, 58
    short-term excitement, 66
    start-up time, 57
    tools, 173
    See also Databases
Command and control structure, 207
Communication
    information chain management facilitation,
        162
    lack of, 162
    organizational structures and, 188
Communications channels, 162, 190–91
Competitive advantage, 47–49
Consumer price index (CPI), 205–6
Consumers
    defined, 35
    needs analysis, 86
Control charts. *See* P-charts
Cost leadership, 46
Costs
    clean-up, 60
    data quality efforts, 59
    error prevention, 60
    poor data quality, 3, 45
    tool, 60
Customer data, 21–25
    importance, 22
    index examples, 24
Customer needs, 23
    analysis process description, 103
    array of, 101
    chain, 102
    changing, 101
    conflicting, 101
    determining, 105
    important, meeting, 105

    spreadsheet, 104
    suppliers and, 105
    translating into requirements, 105
    understanding, 101–6
Customer requirements, 125
    communication of, 144
    control and conformance to, 127
    deploying, to original sources, 142
    improvements to meet, 129
Customers
    common definition of, 23, 24
    complaints, 107
    data quality and, 73
    definition of, 194
    field tips bearing on, 212
    inaccurate data and, 74
    intimacy, effective strategy for, 46
    intimacy, pursuing, 22
    requirements and feedback channels,
        96–97
Customer satisfaction
    measurements, 110
    poor data quality impact on, 45
Customer-Supplier Model, 95–97
    defined, 95
    features, 95
    illustrated, 96
    individual viewpoint, 97
    organization viewpoint, 97
    requirements and feedback channels,
        96–97
    roles, 95–96
    supplier's perspective, 96
Cycle time, 115
    histogram, 117
    measurements, 110

D

Data
    customer, 21–25
    data resource, 28–30

expected lifetime, 61, 63
features, 74
field tips on nature of, 216
interrelated components, 71
modeling, 33, 71
new, sources, 151
as organic, 61
ownership, 184, 185
uses, 73
utility, 62
Databases
clean-up, 54–55
lake analogy, 53–56
polluted, 54
of record (DBOR), 83
Data councils, 177–78
defined, 177
as DQS element, 79
responsibilities, 177–78
role, 182–84
See also Senior leadership
Data creation rate, 61, 62
example, 61–62
importance, 63
measuring, 61
time-series plot, 62
Data culture, advancing, 179, 197–201
Data editing, 89, 120–21
defined, 55
employing, 121
in-chain, 121
principles of, 121
use of, 120
Data entry clerks, 134–35
Data flow, 207–8
across departmental/organizational
boundaries, 207
reorganizing horizontally, 164
Data policy, 181–85
as DQS element, 80
essential elements of, 183

good, 184
issues, 182
Data products
defined, 73
evolution, 206
Data publishers, 10–13
commitment guideline, 13
consumer trust, 10, 13
content guideline, 11
data quality statements, 10–11
improvement guideline, d, 12
presentation guideline, 12
privacy guideline, 11
quality of values guideline, 12
strategies, 10
summary guidelines for, 11–13
Data quality
approaches to, 76
business case for, 37–49
CEOs and, 3–5
CFOs and, 15
CIOs and, 27–34
competitive advantage through, 47–49
customers and, 73
data publishers and, 10–13
data user expectations, 8–9
defined, 73
definition illustration, 74
dimensions, 106
disasters, 39–41
goals definition, 201
impact activities, 72
infancy, 205
levels, 45
management ignorance/misconceptions,
192
organizing for, 187–88
responsibility, 189–90
stakes, 1–2
See also Poor data quality; quality
improvement; Quality planning

Data quality problems, 40
  identifying, 46
  root of, 135
Data quality systems (DQSs), 75–93
  business case, 80
  common elements, 78
  components, 75
  components illustration, 93
  consumer needs analysis, 86
  databases of record (DBOR), 83
  data quality council, 79
  data quality policy, 80
  data quality vision, 79
  data supplier management, 81
  defined, 75
  document assurance, 91
  domain knowledge of data/information, 91
  first-generation, 75
  identification of information chains, 85
  information chain (re)design, 88
  information chain description, 85
  information chain management, 81
  innovation, 82
  inspection and test, 89
  management of data culture, 83
  measurement, 86
  quality assurance, 89
  quality control, 87
  quality handbook, 92
  quality improvement, 88
  quality planning, 87
  rewards and recognition, 90
  second-generation, 75–93
  standardization, 82
  standards, 92
  strategic data quality management, 84
  third-generation, 76
  training and education, 84
Data quality vision (DQS element), 79
Data records
  flawed, 110

  presentation of, 73
  time stamps, 114–15
  tracked, 114
Data repositories, 171
  defined, 173
  interface, 173
Data resource data, 28–30, 67
  answers, 28–29
  chain illustration, 30
  data model description, 28
  data suppliers, 33
  defined, 28, 73
  end-to-end chain, 33
Data suppliers. *See* Suppliers
Data tracking, 113–18
  chain illustration, 116
  choosing, 118
  defined, 113
  information chain illustration, 113
  record example, 114
  time stamps, 114–15
Data users
  commitment expectation, 9
  content expectation, 8
  demands, 7
  improvement expectation, 9
  presentation expectation, 9
  privacy expectation, 8
  quality of values expectation, 9
  summary expectations, 8–9
  trust of data publishers, 13
Data values, 71
Data warehouses, 30–32
  building data quality into, 33
  CIOs and, 31–32
  existing data, 32
  implementation challenges, 31
  migrating data to, 66
  operational sources, 31
  poor data quality impact on, 45

supplier manager, 32
time for data quality, 34
Decision chains
defined, 167
end-to-end, 168
evolution, 170
generic, 168, 169
illustrated, 169
Decision makers, 36, 170
Decision-making
better, 167–70
chains, 151
impacts to, 110
implementation, 168
management, 170
poor data quality impact on, 45, 47
questions, 167
trusted data and, 48
Disasters, 39–41
Document assurance (DQS element), 91
Domain knowledge of data/information
(DQS element), 91
Dot.coms. *See* Data publishers

E

Edit controls, 99, 119–21
creating/applying, 120
defined, 119
use illustration, 120
Error detection engines, 172
Error prevention, 55–56, 57
adopting, 65
before clean-up, 65–66
conclusions, 57
costs, 60
focus, 65
quality levels, 59
start-up time, 57
Error rates
result summaries, 116
time series plots, 124

Errors
correction, 54, 56
finding, 56
histogram of, 116
root causes of, 55
See also Clean-up

F

Features, data, 74
Feedback channel, 96–97
Field tips, 209–16
bearing on customers, 212
for building business case for data quality,
211
for managing/improving data quality,
212–13
most import, 210
on nature of data, 216
on role of technology, 215
overview, 209
for reorganizing/handling social issues, 214
for supplier data quality, 215
Force-field analysis, 198

H

Handoffs, minimizing, 163
High data quality
CEOs and, 4
competition and, 4
determination, 74
different sources and, 141
See also Data quality

I

In-chain editing, 121
Information chain design, 88, 141–45
before supporting information technology,
145
data design, 144
embedded "inspect and work" loops
within, 148–49

Information chain design *(cont'd.)*
  error handling, 144
  for facilitating continuous improvement,
      145
  measurements, 144
  overall focus, 143
  principles, 143–44
  reengineered, 149
  science of, 143
Information chain management, 17, 77, 151,
      161–65
  application, 151
  communication and, 162
  cycle, 161, 162
  as DQS element, 81
  effectiveness, 163
  implementation of, 161
  senior leadership support, 178
  teams, 187
  threatening nature of, 163
Information chains
  critical, 161, 165
  crossing many departments, 164
  defined, 76–77
  description, 85
  examples, 77
  existing, 141
  identification of, 85
  illustrated, 77
  internal, 151
  poorly defined, 200, 201
  quality planning, 142
  supplier, 161
  types of, 61
Information technology (IT)
  applied to poor information chain, 199
  fear of, 192–93
  field tips on role of, 215
In-line editors, 171, 172–73
  applying, 173
  defined, 172

editing procedure, 173
  See also Tools
Innovation (DQS element), 82
Inspection and test (DQS element), 89

K

Knowledge management, 206

L

Lake analogy, 53–56

M

Management of data culture (DQS element),
      83
Marketing managers, customer knowledge,
      21–25
Measurements, 107–8
  baseline, 137–38
  before taking, 111
  benefits, 107
  chain, 108
  customer satisfaction, 110
  cycle time, 110
  data accuracy, 110
  data tracking, 113–18
  as DQS element, 86
  power, 107
  productivity, 110
  results presentation, 111
  summaries, 116
  in supplier management, 156
  top-line summary results, 109
  use of, 107–8
Measurement tools, 171–72
  defined, 171
  spreadsheet automation, 172
  See also Tools
Middle management, 35, 151–73
  information chain management threat to,
      163

resistance to information chain
    management, 165
roles and responsibilities, 151–73

N

Non–value-added work, 111, 162
    defined, 77
    time, 117
    See also Value-added work
Normalization changes, 115

O

Operations, 167
    changes, 115
    poor data quality impact on, 45
    quality levels, 58
Organizational structures, 187–88
    communication, 188
    illustrated, 188
    levels, 187
    needed, 188
Organizations
    cost conscious, 197
    customer focus, 197
    high-technology, 197
    hypothetical, example, 198
    relationships between, 199
Overbilling, 16–17, 44

P

Paradigms, 76
Partnership, 155, 159
P-charts
    creation/use steps, 126
    desired look of, 127
    illustrated, 124
    out-of-control situation, 128
    reestablished control, 129
    using, 129
    See also Statistical control

Poor data quality
    CEOs and, 3–4
    costs, 3
    havoc, 4
    in health industry, 40
    impact of, 35–36, 45
    industry examples, 40–41
    insidious nature of, 43–46
    reengineering and, 149
    See also Data quality
Prevention. *See* Error prevention
Price leaders, 22
Privacy, 206–7, 208
Productivity measurements, 110, 111
Product leadership strategy, 46
Project management tool, 171, 172

Q

Quality assurance (DQS element), 89
Quality control (DQS element), 87
Quality handbook (DQS element), 92
Quality improvement, 99, 131–35
    approach, crafting, 65–67
    charter, 134
    completion tips, 133
    continuous, 135
    costs, 59
    cycle, 131, 132
    defined, 131
    as DQS element, 88
    field tips for, 212–13
    incremental, 131, 147
    methods, 51–56
    outcomes, 57–60
    owner work on, 132–34
    project-by-project approach, 147
    project definition, 135
    project results, 135
    rate of, 138
    reengineering and, 131
    rules, 66

Quality improvement *(cont'd.)*
    self-funding, 63
    simple elegance of, 135
    team, 134
Quality levels
    database clean-up, 58
    error prevention, 59
    measurement, 99
    ongoing operations, 58
Quality planning, 99, 137–45
    chain, 142
    defined, 137
    designing information chains, 141–45
    as DQS element, 87
    immediate progress, 137
    long-term, dramatic progress, 138
    targets, 137
    targets, setting, 137–39
Queue time, minimizing, 163

R

Records. *See* Data records
Reengineering, 131, 147–49
    importance, 147
    out-of-favor factors, 147
    poor data quality and, 149
    as quality improvement methodology
        extension, 148
    situations for, 148
    teams, 149
    warnings, 148
Requirements channel, 96–97
    establishing, 101
    illustrated, 96
Rewards and recognition (DQS element), 90
Root cause analysis, 131–35

S

Scalability, 173
Scorecard tools, 171

Senior leadership, 175–201
    data councils, 177–78
    importance of, 179
    need for, 175
    roles and responsibilities, 178–79
    support and, 177–79
Social issues, 189–95
    battles that can't be won, 193–94
    change takes time/effort, 193
    communications channels, 190–91
    data ownership, 190
    data quality management ignorance/
        misconceptions, 192
    data quality responsibility, 189–90
    field tips for handling, 214
    IT fear, 192–93
    "quality" negative images, 193
Spreadsheets
    automation, 172
    customer needs, 104
    for error rate estimation, 109
Standardization (DQS element), 82
Standards
    chains, 33
    as DQS element, 92
Statistical control, 99, 123–29
    defined, 123
    management activities, 127
    out-of-control situation, 128
    p-charts, 124
    special cause search, 128
    See also P-charts
Statistical Process Control (SPC), 123
Statistical tools, 171, 172
Strategic data quality management (DQS
        element), 84
Supplier management, 17, 151, 153–59
    accountability, 154, 159
    applying, 152, 159
    approaches, 155
    benefits, 153

certification process, 158
concerns, 157–58
cycle, 156
data accuracy, 23
as DQS element, 81
issues, 156–57
partnership, 155, 159
proactive customer-supplier relationship, 155
protection and, 158
quality baselining/ongoing reporting, 155
rewards/penalties, 155
senior leadership support, 178
status quo, 155
steps, 156
Suppliers
critical, 157, 159
customer needs and, 105
Customer-Supplier Model, 96
data quality field tips, 215
data resource data, 33
external, 151
important, 157
large number of, 157
requirements and feedback channels, 97
unimportant, 157

T

Tactics, 167
Targets
baseline, 138
to complete clean-up activity, 138
completed project, 139
current performance and, 137
easy-to-quantify, 137
recommendation, 137
setting, 137–39
See also Quality planning

Time stamps, 114–15
Tool costs, 60
Tools, 152, 171–74
choosing, 174
clean-up, 173
data repositories, 171, 173
essential, 171
in-line editors, 171, 172–73
measurement, 171–72
project management, 171, 172
scorecard, 171
statistical, 171, 172
workflow, 171, 172
Training and education (DQS element), 84
Translation changes, 115
Trivariate domains, 119
Trust, 47
Trusted data, 48

U

Underbilling, 16, 19
Univariate domains, 119

V

Value-added work, 111
defined, 77
time, 117
See also Non–value-added work

W

Workflow tools, 171, 172